Nick Vandome

iPad
for Seniors

in
easy steps

Covers iPad 2 and the new iPad

In easy steps is an imprint of In Easy Steps Limited
4 Chapel Court · 42 Holly Walk · Leamington Spa
Warwickshire · United Kingdom · CV32 4YS
www.ineasysteps.com

Notice of Liability
Every effort has been made to ensure that this book contains accurate
and current information. However, In Easy Steps Limited and the
author shall not be liable for any loss or damage suffered by readers
as a result of any information contained herein.

Trademarks
All trademarks are acknowledged as belonging to their respective
companies.

In Easy Steps Limited supports The Forest Stewardship Council (FSC),
the leading international forest certification organisation. All our titles
that are printed on Greenpeace approved FSC certified paper carry the
FSC logo.

MIX
Paper from
responsible sources
FSC® C020837

FSC
www.fsc.org

Printed and bound in the United Kingdom

ISBN 978-1-84078-536-4

Contents

Knowing Your Apps 63

Keeping in Touch 79

On a Web Safari 95

1 Choosing Your iPad

It's small, it's stylish, it's powerful, and it's perfect for anyone, of any age. This chapter introduces the iPad and covers the basics so you can quickly get up and running with this exciting tablet computer.

The iEverything

The iPad is a tablet computer that has gone a long way to change how we think of computers and how we interact with them. Instead of a large, static, object it is effortlessly mobile and even makes a laptop seem bulky by comparison.

But even with its compact size, the iPad still manages to pack in a lot of power and functionality into its diminutive body. In this case, small is very definitely beautiful and the range of what you can do with the iPad is considerable:

- Communicate via email, video and text messaging

- Surf the Web wirelessly

- Add an endless number of new 'apps' from the Apple App Store

- Use a range of entertainment tools, covering music, photos, video, books and games

- Do all of your favorite productivity tasks such as word processing, creating spreadsheets or producing presentations

- Organize your life with apps for calendars, address books, notes, reminders and much more

Add to this up to 10 hours battery life when you are on the move, a Retina Display screen of outstanding clarity and a seamless backup system and it is clear why the iPad can fulfil all of your computing needs.

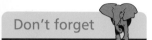
Don't forget

The latest version of the iPad is the third generation. It comes in either white or black.

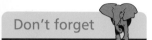
Don't forget

'Apps' is just a fancy name for what are more traditionally called programs in the world of computing. The iPad has several apps that come built-in and ready for use. There are thousands more available for downloading from the online App Store.

Simplicity of the iPad

Computers have become a central part of our everyday lives, but there is no reason why they need to be complex devices that have us scratching our heads as to how to best use them. The iPad is not only stylish and compact, it also makes the computing process as simple as possible, so you can concentrate on what you want to do. Some ways in which this is done are:

- Instantly on. With the iPad there is no long wait for it to turn on, or wake from a state of sleep. When you turn it on, it is ready to use, it's as simple as that

- Apps. iPad apps sit on the home screen, visible and ready to use. Most apps are created in a similar format, so once you have mastered getting around them you will be comfortable using most apps

- Settings. One of the built-in iPad apps is for Settings. This is a one-stop shop for customizing the way that your iPad looks and operates and also how settings for apps work

Hot tip

Much of the way you navigate around the iPad is done by tapping, or swiping, with your fingers, rather than with a traditional keyboard and mouse. There is also a virtual keyboard for input functions.

Don't forget

The Dock is the bar at the bottom of the iPad screen, onto which apps can be placed for quick access.

- Dock and Multitasking Bar. These are two functions that enable you to quickly access your favorite apps, regardless of what you are doing on your iPad

- Home button. This enables you to return to the main home screen at any time. It also has some additional functionality, depending on how many times you click it

The Right Version for You

The iPad is now in its third generation. Following iPad 1 and iPad 2, this is now known by just the title iPad. There are two different versions of the iPad:

- With Wi-Fi connectivity. This enables you to connect to the Internet via a Wi-Fi router, either in your own home, or at a Wi-Fi hotspot

- With Wi-Fi and 4G connectivity (where available, but it also covers 3G)

Each version also has different levels of storage and so the decision as to which one is right for you will largely be based on the following:

- Will you need it to connect to the Internet when you are using it on the move. If not, then the standard model with Wi-Fi should be sufficient

- Will you want to download a lot of music, videos, books and photos on your iPad. The more of these that you use, the more storage you will need. You can monitor the amount of storage that you have used, and with what, within the Settings>General>Usage>Storage section. This displays the amount of storage used by each app:

General	Usage	
Storage		
6.9 GB Available		6.9 GB Used
GarageBand		753 MB >
Music		681 MB >
Numbers		209 MB >
Keynote		175 MB >
Pages		155 MB >
IntellectivePhysics		154 MB >
Guardian iPad edition		140 MB >
iMovie		96.6 MB >

Specifications

The specifications for the iPad are:

- Height: 9.50 inches (241.2 mm), width: 7.31 inches (185.7 mm), depth: 0.37 inch (9.4 mm)

- Processor: Dual-core Apple A5X custom-designed, high-performance, low-power system-on-a-chip with quad-core graphics

- Storage: 16GB, 32GB or 64GB of in-built flash storage

- Wireless: Wi-Fi (802.11a/b/g/n), Bluetooth 4.0

- Screen: Retina Display, 9.7-inch (diagonal) LED-backlit glossy widescreen Multi-Touch display with IPS technology, 2048 by 1536 pixel resolution at 264 pixels per inch (ppi), fingerprint-resistant oleophobic coating

- Battery power: Up to 10 hours of surfing the Web on Wi-Fi, watching video, or listening to music

- Battery charging: Via power adapter (supplied) or USB to computer system

- Input/Output: 30-pin dock connector port, 3.5 mm stereo headphone minijack, built-in speaker, microphone and micro-SIM card tray (Wi-Fi + 4G model only)

- Sensors: Accelerometer, ambient light sensor and gyroscope

- TV and video: AirPlay Mirroring to Apple TV for viewing content on an HDTV

- Mail attachment support: The following file formats can be opened or viewed through the Mail app: .jpg, .tiff, .gif (images); .doc and .docx (Microsoft Word); .htm and .html (web pages); .key (Keynote); .numbers (Numbers); .pages (Pages); .pdf (Preview and Adobe Acrobat); .ppt and .pptx (Microsoft PowerPoint); .txt (text); .rtf (rich text format); .vcf (contact information); .xls and .xlsx (Microsoft Excel)

Beware

Even if you initially think you will not use a lot of storage, this may change once you have bought your iPad. If possible, buy a version with as much storage as possible.

Hot tip

To connect your iPad to an HDTV you will need an Apple Digital AV Adapter or an Apple VGA Adapter (both sold separately).

Before You Switch On

The external controls for the iPad are simple and uncomplicated. Three of them are situated at the top of the iPad and the other is in the middle at the bottom. There are also two cameras, one on the front and one on the back of the iPad.

Controls

The controls at the top of the iPad are:

On/Off button

Side Switch for silent mode (this applies to system sounds rather than the volume of items such as music or videos)

Volume Up or Down button

Cameras. One is located on the back, underneath the On/Off button and one on the front, top

Home button. Press this once to wake up the iPad or return to the Home screen at any point:

Speaker. The speaker is located on the bottom of the iPad:

Dock cable connector. Connect the dock cable here to charge the iPad, or connect it to another computer

Don't forget

To tun on the iPad, press and hold the On/Off button for a few seconds. It can also be used to Sleep the iPad or Wake it from the Sleep state.

Hot tip

The Side Switch can also be used to lock the rotation of the iPad screen. For details about this see Chapter Two page 26.

Don't forget

The third generation iPad has an iSight camera on the back, which is a 5-megapixel camera which can also capture video in HD.

Getting Started

To start using the iPad, press the On/Off button once and hold it down for a few seconds.

Initially there will be a series of setup screens to move through before you can use the iPad:

1 Drag this slider to the right to start the setup process. (This is done by dragging the slider with one finger)

Hot tip

If your iPad ever freezes, or if something is not working properly, it can be rebooted by holding down the Home button and the On/Off button for ten seconds and then turning it on again by pressing and holding the Home button.

13

2 After each step of the setup process, tap once on this arrow in the top right-hand corner, or the Next button

Beware

Some people are uneasy about revealing their location via their iPad. However, it is a useful function that can be used constructively by a number of apps. If you are uncomfortable about it though it can be disabled.

The setup process covers the following items:

- Language. Select the language you want to use

- Country. Select the country in which you are located

- Location Services. This determines whether your iPad can use your geographical location for apps that require this type of information (such as Maps)

- Wi-Fi network. Select a Wi-Fi network to connect to the Internet. If you are at home, this will be your own Wi-Fi network, if available. If you are at a Wi-Fi hotspot then this will appear on your network list

...cont'd

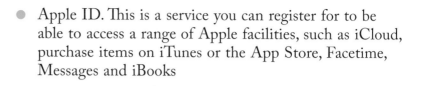

- Apple ID. This is a service you can register for to be able to access a range of Apple facilities, such as iCloud, purchase items on iTunes or the App Store, Facetime, Messages and iBooks

Don't forget

For details about obtaining an Apple ID see Chapter Five.

Don't forget

For more information about using iCloud see Chapter Two.

- iCloud. This is Apple's online service for sharing and backing up content. You have to register for iCloud, with an Apple ID, and once you have done this you can specify which items you want to be made available to other compatible devices via iCloud

- Find My iPad. This is a service that can be activated so that you can locate your iPad if it is lost or stolen. This is done via the online iCloud site at www.icloud.com

Hot tip

The Find My iPad function can also be set up within the Location Services and iCloud sections of the Settings app.

- Dictation. If this is turned on, a microphone icon on the virtual keyboard can be used to enter text by speaking rather than typing

- Diagnostic information. This enables information about your iPad to be sent to Apple

- Register. This enables you to register your iPad with Apple so you are the registered owner

- Start using. Once the setup process has been completed you can start using your iPad

Home Screen

Once you have completed the setup process you will see the Home screen of the iPad. This contains the built-in apps:

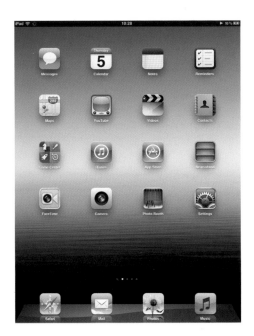

Don't forget

Items on the Dock can be removed and new ones can be added. For more details about this, see Chapter Two.

At the bottom of the screen are four apps that appear by default in the Dock area.

Rotate the iPad and the orientation changes automatically.

Home Button

The Home button, located at the bottom, middle on the iPad, can be used to perform a number of tasks:

 Click once on the Home button to return to the Home screen at any point

 Double-click on the Home button to access the Multitasking Bar. This is at the bottom of the screen and shows the most recently used and open apps. The rest of the Home screen is greyed out. Tap once on an app to access it

Don't forget

For more information about using the iPad search facility, see Chapter Two.

Click once on the Home button when on the Home screen to access the iPad search function

Opening Items

All apps on your iPad can be opened with the minimum of fuss and effort:

 Tap once on an icon to open the app

 The app opens at its home screen

Don't forget

For details about closing items see Chapter Two.

3 Click once on the Home button to return to the Home screen

Hot tip

If you access the Multitasking Bar from the Home screen it will display all of the open apps. If you access it from another app, it will display all of the open apps, bar the one which you currently have open.

4 Access the Multitasking Bar as shown on the previous page. All open apps are shown here. Tap once on an icon to access that app again

Charging Your iPad

The iPad comes with a Dock Connector to USB Cable and a USB Power Adapter. These can be used to charge the iPad:

1 Connect the USB end of the Dock Connector cable to the Power Adapter

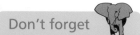

Don't forget

The Dock Connector cable can also be used to connect your iPad to a separate Dock. This is a unit that can be used as a stand for the iPad and also charge it too.

2 Connect the other end of the Dock Connector cable to the iPad

3 Plug in the Power Adapter

The iPad can also be charged by connecting it with the Dock Connector cable to another computer. However, this has to be another Mac computer and, if it is a MacBook, it has to be plugged in too for the iPad to charge.

2 Around Your iPad

Once you have turned on your iPad you will want to start using it as soon as possible. This chapter shows how to do this with details about settings, navigation, accessibility features and also registering for and setting up the iCloud service for sharing your content.

iPad Settings

The Settings app is the one that should probably be explored first as it controls settings for the appearance of the iPad and the way it, and its apps, operate. To use the Settings app:

 Tap once on the Settings app icon

 The Settings are listed down the left-hand side and the options are shown on the right-hand side

Don't forget

If a Settings option has an On/Off button next to it, this can be changed by swiping the button to either the left or right.

Tap on a link to see additional options for that item

Tap once here to move back to the main category for the selected Setting

The System Settings are:

- Airplane Mode. This can be used while on an airplane

- Wi-Fi. This enables you to select a wireless network. Available networks will be displayed here

- Notifications. This determines how the Notification Center operates in terms of alerting the user to different types of notifications

- Location Services. This can be used to specify settings for determining the location of your iPad

- Brightness & Wallpaper. This can be used to set the screen brightness manually or automatically and select a wallpaper

- Picture Frame. This can activate your iPad as a picture frame when it is locked

- General. This contains a number of settings for how the iPad operates. This is one of the most useful Settings

- iCloud. This contains settings for items that are to be saved to the online iCloud

Hot tip

To change the iPad's wallpaper, tap once on the arrow next to the iPad icon in the Brightness & Wallpaper Setting. From here you can select system images, or ones that you have taken yourself and saved on your iPad.

21

iCloud

iCloud	
Account	nickvandome@mac.com >
Mail	ON
Contacts	ON
Calendars	ON

...cont'd

- Mail, Contacts, Calendars. This has options for how these three apps operate

- Twitter. Use this to install Twitter and create an account

- FaceTime. This is used to turn video calling On or Off

- Safari. Settings for the Safari Web browser

Beware

If you turn on Private Browsing within the Safari Settings, no record of visited Web pages will be kept.

Safari	
General	
Search Engine	Google >
AutoFill	Names and Passwords >
Open New Tabs in Background	OFF
Always Show Bookmarks Bar	ON
Privacy	
Private Browsing	OFF
Accept Cookies	From visited >

- Messages. This can be used to sign-in to the Messages app for sending and receiving text messages

- Music. This has options for how you listen to music

- Videos. This has options for how you view videos

- Photos. This has options for viewing and editing photos, slideshow settings and options for uploading to iCloud

Photos	
Photo Stream	
Photo Stream	ON
Photo Stream automatically uploads new photos to iCloud and downloads them to all of your devices when connected to Wi-Fi.	
Slideshow	
Play Each Slide For	3 Seconds >
Repeat	OFF
Shuffle	OFF

- Notes. This contains formatting options for creating items in the Notes app

- Store. This can be used to specify downloading options from the iTunes Store and the App Store, for music, books and apps

Using the Dock

By default, there are four apps on the Dock, at the bottom of the screen. These are the four that it is thought you will use most frequently:

- Safari, for Web browsing

- Mail, for email

- Photos

- Music

You can rearrange the order in which the Dock apps appear:

 Tap and hold on one of the Dock apps until it starts to jiggle

2 Drag the app into its new position

3 Click once on the Home button to return from edit mode

Hot tip

Just above the Dock is a small magnifying glass icon and a number of small dots. The magnifying glass can be used to access the Search function, by tapping on it once. The dots indicate how many screens of content there are on the iPad. Tap on one of the dots to go to that screen.

...cont'd

Adding and removing Dock apps

You can also remove apps from the Dock and add new ones:

 To remove an app from the Dock tap and hold it and drag it onto the main screen area

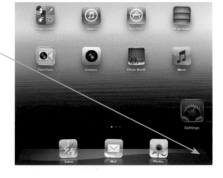

Don't forget

If items are removed from the Dock they are still available in the same way from the main screen.

2 To add an app to the Dock tap and hold it and drag it onto the Dock

3 The number of items that can be added to the Dock is restricted to a maximum of six as the icons do not resize themselves

4 Click once on the Home button to return from edit mode

Multitasking Bar

The Multitasking Bar can be accessed at the bottom of the screen and it performs a number of tasks:

- Shows open apps

- Allows access to music and video controls

- Allows screen rotation to be locked

- Enables apps to be closed

Accessing the Multitasking Bar
The Multitasking Bar can be accessed in two ways:

 Double-click on the Home button

 Swipe up, from the bottom of the screen, with four or five fingers

Don't forget

The Multitasking Bar can be accessed from either the Home screen or any open app. To exit the Multitasking Bar, tap once on the main screen, or click once on the Home button to return to the Home screen.

 Swipe left and right to view the items on the Multitasking Bar

...cont'd

Accessing Controls
To access the music and video controls:

1 Swipe from left to right on the Multitasking Bar

2 Use the controls to, from left to right, rewind a song or video, play a song or video, fast forward a song or video, adjust the volume of a song or video

Hot tip

The screen rotation can also be locked from within the General section of the Settings app. Under 'Use Side Switch to:', tap once on the Lock Rotation link. Then the side switch can be used to lock, and unlock, the screen rotation. If this is selected, the button in Step 2 can be used to mute the system volume instead.

Locking screen rotation
The Multitasking Bar can also be used to lock the screen rotation so that the orientation stays the same regardless of how you move the iPad. To do this:

1 Swipe from left to right on the Multitasking Bar

2 Tap once on this icon

3 The padlock icon indicates that the screen rotation is locked

Closing Items

The iPad deals with open apps very efficiently. They do not interact with other apps, which increases security and also means that they can be open in the background without using up a significant amount of processing power, in a state of semi-hibernation, until they are needed. Because of this it is not essential to close apps when you move to something else. However, you may want to do this to clear up the Multitasking Bar, or if an app stops working. To do this:

1. Access the Multitasking Bar. Tap and hold on an app until the icon starts to jiggle and a red circle appears in the left-hand corner

2. Tap once on the red circle to close the app

3. The app is removed from the Multitasking Bar

4. The app is only closed, not removed from your iPad. It is still accessible from the Home screen and when you open it again it will be available on the Multitasking Bar too

Don't forget

When you switch from one app to another, the first one stays open in the background. You can go back to it by accessing it from the Multitasking Bar or the Home screen.

Navigating Around

Most of the navigation on the iPad is done with Multi-Touch Gestures, which are looked at on the next three pages. Two of these can also be used for basic navigation:

Swiping between screens

Once you have added more apps to your iPad they will start to fill up more screens. To move between these:

Swipe left or right with one, or two, fingers.

Don't forget

You can also move between different screens by tapping once on the small dots in the middle of the screen above the Dock.

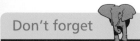

Don't forget

You can also return to the Home screen by clicking once on the Home button.

Returning to the Home screen

Pinch together with thumb and four fingers to return to the Home screen from any open app.

Swipe, Tap and Pinch

Since there is no mouse connected to the iPad, navigation is done with the user's fingers. There are a combination of tapping, swiping and pinching gestures that can be used to view items such as Web pages, photos, maps and documents and also navigate around the iPad.

Swiping up and down
Swipe up and down with one finger to move up or down Web pages, photos, maps or documents. The content moves in the opposite direction of the swipe i.e. if you swipe up the page will move down and vice versa.

Hot tip

The faster you swipe on the screen, the faster the screen moves up or down.

Tapping and zooming
Double-tap with one finger to zoom in on a Web page, photo, map or document. Double-tap with two fingers to return to the original view.

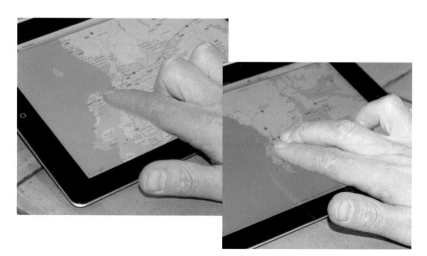

...cont'd

Pinching and swiping

Swipe outwards with thumb and forefinger to zoom in on a Web page, photo, map or document.

Don't forget

Swiping outwards with thumb and forefinger enables you to zoom in on an item to a greater degree than double-tapping with one finger.

Pinch together with thumb and forefinger to zoom back in on a Web page, photo, map or document.

More gestures

- Swipe left or right with four or five fingers to move between open apps

- Swipe up with four or five fingers to reveal the Multitasking Bar at the bottom of the screen

- Drag with two or three fingers to move a Web page, photo, map or document

- Swipe left or right with one finger to move between full size photos in the Photos app

- Tap once on a photo thumbnail with one finger to enlarge it to full screen within the Photos app

- Tap once with two fingers on a full size photo to reduce it to a thumbnail within the Photos app

- Drag down at the top-middle of the iPad to view current notifications in the Notifications Center

Hot tip

The gestures involving four or five fingers can be turned On or Off in the General section of the Settings app.

31

Searching With Spotlight

Spotlight is the search facility that is provided with the iPad. It can be accessed from the main Home screen by clicking once on the Home button.

Spotlight can search for apps on your iPad and also search for items within the following apps:

- Calendar
- Contacts
- Mail
- Messages
- Music, video, podcasts and audiobooks
- Notes
- Reminders

To search for items with Spotlight:

Don't forget

To return to the Home screen from the Search page, click once on the Home button.

1 Type the search keywords into the search box

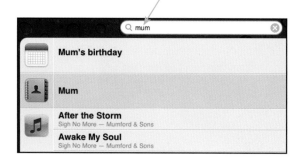

2 Tap once on one of the results

3 Tap once on these buttons to search for the item over the Web or Wikipedia

Launching apps with Spotlight

Once you have downloaded a lot of apps, and they are on several screens, Spotlight can be a good way to quickly find and launch specific apps. To do this:

 Enter the name, or part of it, of the app into the search box

2 Tap once on the app name to launch it

Spotlight settings

Within the Settings app you can select which items the Spotlight search operates over. To do this:

1 Tap once on the Settings app

2 Tap once on General tab

General

3 Tap once on the Spotlight Search link

Spotlight Search

4 Tap once on an item to exclude it from the Spotlight search

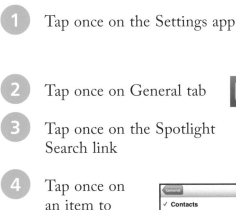

Hot tip

If you hide the keyboard when on the Search page, the Dock items become visible and can be selected. For details on hiding the keyboard, see Chapter Three.

33

Accessibility Issues

The iPad tries to cater to as wide a range of users as possible, including those who have difficulty with vision, hearing or physical and motor issues. There are a number of settings that can help with these areas. To access the range of accessibility settings:

1 Tap once on the Settings app

2 Tap once on General tab

General

3 Tap once on the Accessibility link

Accessibility	>

4 The settings for Vision, Hearing and Physical & Motor are displayed here

General	Accessibility	
Vision		
VoiceOver		Off >
Zoom		Off >
Large Text		Off >
White on Black		OFF
Speak Selection		Off >
Speak Auto-text		OFF
Automatically speak auto-corrections and auto-capitalizations.		
Hearing		
Mono Audio		OFF
L ———————————⚬——————— R		
Physical & Motor		
AssistiveTouch		Off >
Triple-click Home		Off >

Vision settings

These can help anyone with impaired vision and there are options for speaking items on the screen and also for making text easier to read:

 1 Tap once on the VoiceOver link

VoiceOver	Off >

2 Drag this button to On to activate the VoiceOver function. This then enables items to be spoken when you tap on them

VoiceOver	ON

VoiceOver speaks items on the screen.

To select an item
Touch it.

To activate the selected item
Double-tap.

To scroll
Flick three fingers.

3 Select options for VoiceOver as required

Speak Hints	ON
Speaking Rate	
🐢 ———————○——————— 🐇	
Typing Feedback	>
Use Phonetics	ON
Use Pitch Change	ON
Use Compact Voice	OFF

Don't forget

When VoiceOver is On, tap once on an item to select it and have it spoken; double-tap to activate the item.

Hot tip

There is a wide range of options for the way VoiceOver can be used. For full details see the Apple website at www.apple.com/ accessibility/ipad/ vision.htm

...cont'd

4 Tap once on the Accessibility button to return to the main options

Accessibility

5 Tap once on these buttons to access options for zooming the screen, increasing text size, showing white text on a black background and speaking of text options

Zoom	Off >
Large Text	Off >
White on Black	OFF
Speak Selection	Off >
Speak Auto-text	OFF

6 Tap once on the Accessibility button to return to the main options after each selection

Hearing settings

These can be used to change the iPad speaker from stereo to mono. To do this:

1 Drag this button to On to enable Mono Audio

Hearing	
Mono Audio	ON
L ———————————— R	

2 Drag this button to specify whether sound all comes out of the left or the right side of the speaker

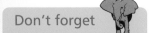

Don't forget

If you turn on the Zoom function you can magnify the whole screen by double-tapping twice. To move around the screen, drag with three fingers. To change the amount of zoom, double-tap with three fingers and drag up or down on the screen.

Hot tip

The Speak Auto-text function can be turned on so that auto-corrections and auto-capitalizations are automatically spoken.

AssistiveTouch

This can be used by anyone who has difficulty navigating around the iPad with the screen or buttons. It can be used with an external device such as a joystick, or it can be used on its own. To use AssistiveTouch:

1 Tap once on the AssistiveTouch link

Physical & Motor	
AssistiveTouch	Off >

2 Drag this button to On to activate the AssistiveTouch function

AssistiveTouch	ON

3 The AssistiveTouch icon appears in the bottom right-hand corner of the screen

4 Tap once on the AssistiveTouch icon to view its options

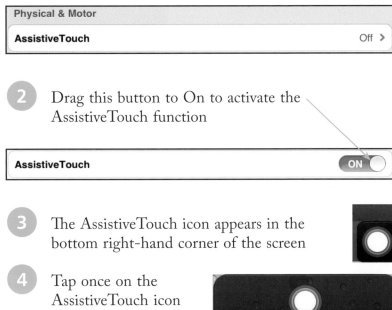

5 Tap once on the Home icon to return to the Home screen

Don't forget

The AssistiveTouch options make it easier for anyone with difficulties clicking the Home button, or using Multi-Touch Gestures.

37

...cont'd

6 Tap once on the Gestures icon to access options for assistance with performing Multi-Touch Gestures

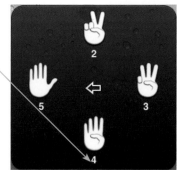

7 Tap once on the number of fingers for the gesture you want to complete

8 The corresponding number of circles appear on the screen

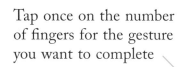

9 Swipe in the required direction for the task i.e. swipe up to access the Multitasking Bar. This is done with one finger, rather than with all of the fingers required for a standard Multi-Touch Gesture

10 Tap once on the Favorites button to access the Pinch gesture and record your own

11 Tap once on the Pinch icon

12 The pinch icon appears on the screen

Hot tip

The Favorites section can also be used to create custom gestures. To do this, tap once on one of the empty boxes and then record the gesture in the New Gesture window. Once it is saved it becomes available in the Favorites section.

13 Tap and drag with one finger on one of the arrows to perform the pinch gesture

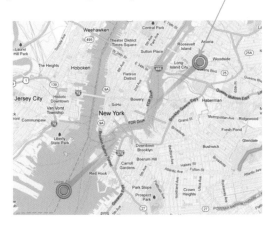

...cont'd

 14 Tap once on the Device icon

 15 Tap once to activate the required function, including changing the screen rotation and adjusting the volume

Triple-click options

The Home button can also be used with a triple-click action to perform a variety of accessibility tasks. To do this:

1 Tap once on the Triple-click Home link

Triple-click Home	Off >

2 Tap once on one of these options to set this as the action for when you triple-click the Home button

Triple-click the Home Button:	
Off	
Toggle VoiceOver	
Toggle White on Black	✓
Toggle Zoom	
Toggle AssistiveTouch	
Ask	

Auto-Locking the Screen

To save power it is possible to set your iPad screen to auto-lock. This is the equivalent of the sleep option on a traditional computer. To do this:

1 Tap once on the Settings app

2 Tap once on the General tab

3 Tap once on the Auto-Lock link

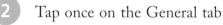
Auto-Lock	Never >

4 Tap once on a duration for when the screen is locked

5 Once the screen is locked, drag this button to the right to unlock the screen

Don't forget

The screen can also be locked by clicking once on the On/Off button at the top of the iPad.

Don't forget

Auto-locking the screen does not prevent other people from accessing your iPad. If you want to prevent anyone else having access, it can be locked with a passcode. See Chapter Twelve for details.

41

Updating Software

The operating system that powers the iPad is known as iOS. This is a mobile computing operating system and it is also used on the iPhone and the iPod Touch. The version on the third generation iPad is 5.1. Periodically, there are updates to the iOS, to fix bugs and add new features. These can be downloaded to your iPad once they are released. To do this:

1 Tap once on the Settings app

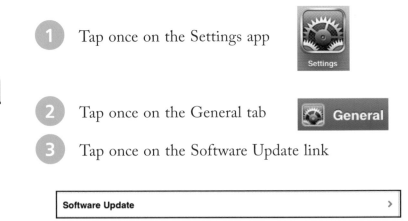

Don't forget

If your iOS software is up to date there is a message to this effect in the Software Update window.

2 Tap once on the General tab

3 Tap once on the Software Update link

Software Update   >

4 If there is an update available it will be displayed here, with details of what is contained within it

Hot tip

It is always worth updating the iOS to keep up to date with fixes. Also, app developers update their products to use the latest iOS features.

5 Tap once on this button to download and install the iOS update. This will then be done automatically

Living in the iCloud

iCloud is the Apple online service that performs a number of valuable functions:

- Makes your content available across multiple devices. The content is stored in the iCloud and then pushed out to other iCloud-enabled devices, including the iPhone, iPod Touch and other Mac or Windows computers

- Enables online access to your content via the iCloud website. This includes your iCloud email, contacts, calendar and reminders

- Backs up the content on your iPad

Once you have registered for and setup iCloud, it works automatically so you do not have to worry about anything. To set up iCloud:

1 You need to have an Apple ID to register for iCloud. See Chapter Five for details about obtaining an Apple ID

2 During the setup process for your iPad, tap once on the Use iCloud link, or

Don't forget

It is free to register and setup a standard iCloud account.

43

Hot tip

To access your iCloud account through the website, access www. icloud.com and enter your Apple ID details.

...cont'd

3 Tap once on the Settings app

4 Tap once on the iCloud tab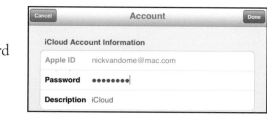

5 Tap once on the Account link

Don't forget

The Account window also has details of your iCloud email account.

iCloud	
Account	nickvandome@mac.com >

6 Enter your Apple ID and password to setup iCloud on your iPad

Cancel	Account	Done
iCloud Account Information		
Apple ID	nickvandome@mac.com	
Password	••••••••	
Description	iCloud	

Beware

By default, you get 5GB of free storage space with an iCloud account. However, there is an introductory offer until a certain date. Make sure you select the Downgrade Options and choose the Free Plan to ensure you do not automatically get put onto a paid-for storage Plan.

7 Tap once here to view your current storage details

Storage Plan
20GB £28.00 / year — 25 GB total iCloud storage >
Payment Information >

8 Upgrade options are displayed. Tap once on this button and then select the free 5GB storage option

Cancel	Change Storage Plan	Buy
Current Plan		
20GB £28.00 / year — 25 GB total iCloud storage		✓
Choose an Upgrade... You will be charged immediately and each year until you change or cancel your plan.		
50GB £70.00 / year — 55 GB total iCloud storage		
Downgrade Options		>

44

iCloud settings

Once you have setup your iCloud account you can then apply settings for how it works. Once you have done this you will not have to worry about it again:

 1 Access the iCloud section in the Settings app, as above

2 Drag these buttons to On for each item that you wish to be included in iCloud. Each item is then saved and stored in the iCloud and made available to your other iCloud-enabled devices

Mail	ON
Contacts	ON
Calendars	ON
Reminders	ON
Bookmarks	ON
Notes	ON
Photo Stream	On >
Documents & Data	On >
Find My iPad	ON

3 Tap once on the Photo Stream and Documents & Data links to access the buttons for turning these On

Photo Stream

Photo Stream ON

Photo Stream automatically uploads new photos to iCloud and downloads them to all of your devices when connected to Wi-Fi.

Documents & Data ON

Allow apps to store documents and data in iCloud.

Don't forget

The Apple iWork apps, Pages, Keynote and Numbers, have their content saved into the iCloud under Documents & Data.

...cont'd

iCloud Storage & Backup

It is possible to view how the storage on your iCloud account is being used and also specify how your content is backed up to iCloud. To do this:

1 Access the iCloud section in the Settings app, as above, and tap once on the Storage & Backup link

2 Tap once on the Manage Storage link to view how your iCloud storage is being used

3 Tap once on an app to view the individual documents within it that are being stored

4 Drag this button to On to enable automatic backups

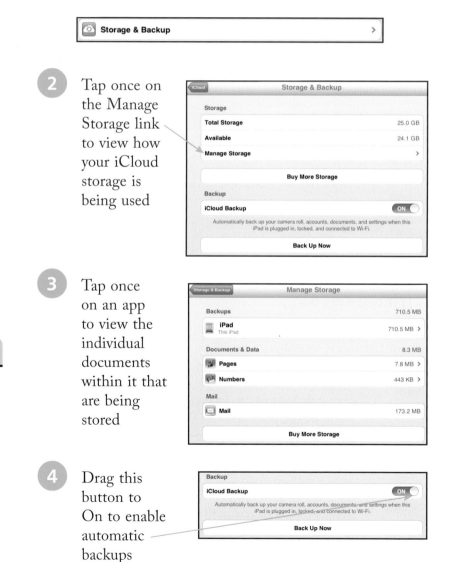

iPad Smart Cover

One of the issues with a touch screen, such as the one on the iPad, is that it is liable to scratch if it is carried around in a bag or even being moved around in the home. The solution to this is an iPad cover (known as a Smart Cover). Being Apple, this not only protects the screen but it is designed so that it can also be used as a stand to support the iPad for viewing content or typing with the keyboard.

There are settings for the iPad cover in the Settings app. This can enable it to lock or unlock the iPad:

 Tap once on the Settings app

2 Tap once on the General tab

3 Under iPad
Cover Lock/
Unlock drag

the button to On to enable the cover to lock or unlock the iPad when it is placed in position or removed

Don't forget

Smart Covers come in a variety of colors and there are also leather ones available.

Attaching the cover

The iPad cover attaches with a hinge along the left-hand side of the iPad. Attach it by placing the hinge on the side of the iPad until it clicks magnetically into place.

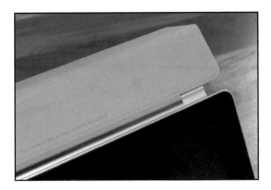

...cont'd

Using the cover as a stand

The iPad cover is separated into four foldable panels. These can be folded into a triangular shape to create a stand for the iPad:

Use the stand at the top of the iPad when using the keyboard for input options:

Use the stand at the bottom of the iPad when viewing content such as videos, photos, books or magazines:

3 The iPad Keyboard

The iPad has a virtual keyboard rather than a traditional one. This chapter shows how to use it and also edit text and add shortcuts.

It's Virtually a Keyboard

The keyboard on the iPad is a virtual one i.e. it appears on the touch screen whenever text or numbered input is required for an app. This can be for a variety of reasons:

- Entering text with a word processing app, email or an organizing app such as Notes

- Entering a Web address in a Web browser such as the Safari app

- Entering information into a form

- Entering a password

Viewing the keyboard

When you attempt one of the items above, the keyboard appears before you can enter any text or numbers:

Around the keyboard

To access the various keyboard controls:

1 Tap once on this button to create a Cap text letter

2 Double-tap on this button to create Caps Lock

3 Tap once on this button to back delete an item

Don't forget

In addition to the iPad virtual keyboard, it is also possible to use a traditional computer keyboard with the iPad. This can be particularly useful if you are using the iPad for a lot of typing. The keyboard is an Apple Wireless Keyboard which connects via Bluetooth. This can be turned on in the General section of the Settings app, under the Bluetooth link.

Don't forget

To return from Caps Lock, tap once on the Caps button.

4 Tap once on this button to access the Numbers keyboard option

5 From the Numbers keyboard, tap once on this button to access the Symbols keyboard

51

6 Tap once on this button on either of the two keyboards above to return to the standard QWERTY option

ABC

7 Tap once on this button to hide the keyboard (this can be done from any of the keyboard options). If the keyboard is hidden, tap once on one of the input options e.g. entering text, to show it again

Keyboard Settings

Settings for the keyboard can be determined in the General section of the Settings app. To do this:

1 Tap once on the Settings app

2 Tap once on the General tab

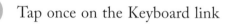

3 Tap once on the Keyboard link

Keyboard	>

4 Drag this slider to On to enable Auto-Capitalization i.e. letters will automatically be capitalized at the beginning of a sentence

Auto-Capitalization	ON

5 Drag this slider to On to enable Auto-Correction i.e. suggestions for words will appear as you type, particularly if you have mis-typed a word

Auto-Correction	ON

6 Drag this slider to On to check spelling as you type

Check Spelling	ON

7 Drag this slider to On to enable the Caps Lock function to be performed

Enable Caps Lock	ON

8 Drag this slider to On to enable shortcut functionality

"." Shortcut	ON

9 Drag this slider to On to enable the keyboard to be split and moved. Tap once on the International Keyboards link to access options for adding different international keyboards

Split Keyboard	ON
International Keyboards	1 >

10 Tap once on this link to view existing text shortcuts and also to create new ones

Shortcuts	
omw	On my way! >
Add New Shortcut...	>

11 Tap once on this link to create new shortcuts

Don't forget

For more information about keyboard shortcuts, see pages 59-61.

53

Entering Text

Once you have applied the keyboard settings that you require you can start entering text. To do this:

 Tap once on the screen to activate the keyboard. Start typing with the keyboard. The text will appear at the point where you tapped on the screen

Don't forget

If you keep typing as normal, the Auto-Correction suggestion will disappear when you finish the word.

 As you type, Auto-Correction comes up with suggestions. Tap once on the spacebar to accept the suggestion, or tap once on the cross next to it to reject it

Remem|
Remember ×

If Check Spelling is enabled, any misspelled words appear underlined in red

Remember to go to the supermrket

 Tap once on this button to hide the keyboard

Editing Text

Once text has been entered it can be selected, copied, cut and pasted. Depending on the app being used, the text can also be formatted, such as with a word processing app.

Selecting text

To select text and perform tasks on it:

1 To change the insertion point, tap and hold until the magnifying glass appears

2 Drag the magnifying glass to move the insertion point

3 Tap once at the insertion point to access the selection buttons

4 Double-tap on a word to select it. Tap once on Cut or Copy as required

5 Drag the selection handles to expand or contract the selection

6 If text has been copied, tap and hold at a new point on the page and tap once on Paste

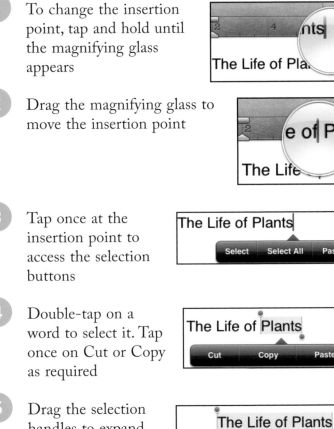

55

Hot tip

Once the selection buttons have been accessed, tap once on Select to select the previous word, or Select All to select all of the text.

...cont'd

Formatting text

Once text has been added to a document it can be formatted in a number of ways (depending on the app). To do this:

1 Select text in a document as shown on the previous page. Instead of copying it, it can be formatted with buttons within the app (this is for the Pages app)

Don't forget

Some apps that allow text entry have formatting options, while others do not and text is just entered in a standard format.

2 Tap once on these buttons to, from left to right, change the font, decrease the font size, set a specific font size and increase the font size

3 Tap once on these buttons to, from left to right, create bold, italic or underlined text or set the text alignment

Moving the Keyboard

By default, the keyboard appears as a single unit along the bottom of the screen. However, it is possible to split the keyboard so that it appears on separate sides of the screen. It is also possible to undock the keyboard and move it around the screen.

Undocking the keyboard
To undock the keyboard from its position at the bottom of the screen:

1 Press and hold on this button on the keyboard

2 Tap once on the Undock button

3 The keyboard is undocked from the bottom of the screen

4 Tap and hold here at the side of the button to move the keyboard

5 The keyboard can then be moved to different positions around the screen

Hot tip

To redock the keyboard, tap and hold on the button in Step 1 and tap once on the Dock button.

...cont'd

Splitting the keyboard

The keyboard can also be split into two and used on either side of the screen. To do this:

 Press and hold on this button on the keyboard

 Tap once on the Split button

 The keyboard is split to the left and the right sides of the screen

Beware

When the keyboard is split, both sides can be a bit small and it is a bit more fiddly than using the full size keyboard.

 Tap and hold here at the side of the button to move the split keyboard

Tap and hold on the button above and tap once on the Dock and Merge button to return the keyboard to its default position at the bottom of the screen

Keyboard Shortcuts

There are two types of shortcuts that can be used on the iPad keyboard:

- Shortcuts on the keys on the keyboard

- Shortcuts created with text abbreviations

Shortcuts with keys

The shortcuts that can be created with the keys on the keyboard are:

1 Double-tap on the spacebar to add a full stop/period and a space at the end of a sentence

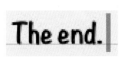

2 Swipe up once on the comma (or press and hold) to insert an apostrophe

3 Swipe up once on the full stop/period to insert quotation marks

4 Press and hold on appropriate letters to access accented versions for different languages

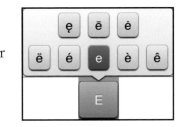

The shortcut in Step 1 can be disabled by switching off the Shortcut option within the Settings>General> Keyboard section.

...cont'd

Text abbreviations

To create shortcuts with text abbreviations:

1 Tap once on the Settings app

2 Tap once on the General tab

3 Tap once on the Keyboard link

Keyboard	>

4 Tap once on the Add New Shortcut... link

Shortcuts

Add New Shortcut...	>

5 Enter the phrase you want to be made into a shortcut

Phrase	My name is Nick

6 Enter the abbreviation you want to use as the shortcut for the phrase

Shortcut	mnn

7 Tap once on the Save button **Save**

8 The shortcut is displayed here

Shortcuts

mnn	My name is Nick >

60

Using shortcuts

Once you have created shortcuts you can then use them with the iPad keyboard. To do this:

1 Enter the abbreviation. As you type, the phrase appears underneath the abbreviation

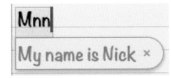

2 Tap once on the spacebar to add the phrase, or tap once on the cross to reject it

Deleting shortcuts

Shortcuts can be deleted, if you do not want to use them anymore. To do this:

1 In the Keyboard section of the General Settings, tap once on the Edit button

2 Tap once on the red circle next to the shortcut you want to delete

Shortcuts

| mnn | My name is Nick |
| omw | On my way |

3 Tap once on the Delete button to remove the shortcut

4 Tap once on the Done button

Hot tip

The shortcut abbreviation is not case sensitive i.e. you can enter it in upper or lower case and the same phrase will appear from the shortcut item.

61

Don't forget

Abbreviation shortcuts work even if the Auto-Correction function has been disabled.

Dictation

On the keyboard there is also a dictation option, which enables you to enter text by speaking into a microphone, rather than typing on the keyboard.

Dictation settings

The dictation function can be turned on during the initial iPad setup process or it can be turned on in the Settings app under the General tab. To do this:

Beware

Dictation is not an exact science and you may find that some strange examples appear. The best results are created if you speak as clearly as possible and reasonably slowly.

1 Tap once on the Keyboard link

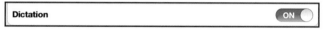
Keyboard	>

2 Drag the Dictation button On

Dictation	ON

Using dictation

Dictation can be used with any app with a text input function. To do this:

Don't forget

There are other dictation apps available from the App Store. Two to try are Dragon Dictation and Voice Dictation.

1 Tap once on this button on the keyboard to activate the dictation microphone. Speak into the microphone to record text

2 As the dictation function is processing the recording these buttons appear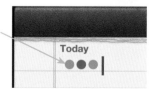

Today
• • •

3 Once the recording has been processed the text appears in app

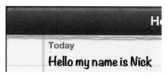
Today
Hello my name is Nick

4 Knowing Your Apps

Apps are the parts that keep the iPad engine running. This chapter details the built-in ones and also shows how to access and use apps from the App Store.

What is an App?

An app is just a more modern name for a computer program. Initially, it was used in relation to mobile devices, such as the iPhone and the iPad, but it is now becoming more widely used with desktop and laptop computers, for both Mac and Windows operating systems.

On the iPad there are two types of apps:

● Built-in apps. These are the apps that come pre-installed on the iPad

● App Store apps. These are apps that can be downloaded from the online App Store. There is a huge range of apps available here, covering a variety of different categories. Some are free while others have to be paid for. The apps here are updated and added to on a daily basis so there are always new ones to explore

64

There are also two important points about apps (both built-in and those from the App Store) to remember:

● Apart from some of the built-in apps, the majority of apps do not interact with each other. This means that there is less chance of viruses being transmitted from app to app on your iPad and they can operate without a reliance on other apps

● Content created by apps is saved within the app itself, rather than within a file structure on your iPad, e.g. if you create a note in the Notes app, it is saved here, if you take a photo, it is saved in the Photos app. Content is usually also saved automatically when it is created, or edited, so you do not have to worry about saving it as you work on it

Built-in Apps

The built-in iPad apps are the ones that appear on the Home screen when you turn on the iPad:

Don't forget

The iPad Settings app is another of the built-in apps and this is looked at in detail in Chapter Two.

- App Store. This can be used to access the App Store, from where additional apps can then be downloaded

- Calendar. An app for storing appointments, important dates and other calendar information

- Contacts. An address book app. Once contacts are added here they can then also be accessed from other apps, such as Mail

- FaceTime. This is an app that uses the built-in FaceTime camera on the iPad to hold video chat with other iPad users, or those with an iPhone, iPod Touch or a Mac computer

Don't forget

Some of the built-in apps, such as Mail and Contacts, interact with each other. However, since these are designed by Apple there is almost no chance of them containing viruses.

...cont'd

Beware

You need an Apple ID to obtain iBooks. They are downloaded in a matter of seconds and you cannot change your mind once you have entered your Apple ID details.

- Games Center. For those who like gaming, this is an app for playing a variety of games, either individually or with friends

- iBooks. This is an app for downloading electronic books, that can then be read on the iPad. This can be done for plain text or illustrated iBooks. Although this is considered a built-in app, it has to first be downloaded from the App Store

- iTunes. This app can be used to browse the iTunes store where music, TV shows, movies and more, can be dowloaded to your iPad

- Mail. This is the email app for sending and receiving email on your iPad

- Maps. Use this app to view maps from around the world, find specific locations and get directions to destinations

- Messages. This is the iPad messaging service, that can be used between iPads, iPhones, iPod Touches and Mac computers. It can be used with not only text but also photos and videos

- Music. An app for playing music on your iPad and also viewing cover artwork. You can also use it to create your own playlists

- Newsstand. Similar to iBooks, this app can be used to download and read newspaper and magazine subscriptions

- Notes. If you need to jot down your thoughts or ideas, this app is perfect for just that

- Photo Booth. A photography app that can be used to create distorted and special effects photos of people or objects

- Photos. This is an app for viewing and editing photos and creating slideshows

- Reminders. Use this app for organization, when you want to create to-do lists and set reminders for events

- Safari. The Apple Web browser that has been developed for viewing the Web on your iPad

- Video. This is an app for viewing videos on your iPad and also streaming them to a larger HDTV monitor

- YouTube. View YouTube videos with this app

About the App Store

While the built-in apps that come with the iPad are flexible and versatile, it really comes into its own when you connect to the App Store. This is an online resource and there are thousands of apps here that can be downloaded and then used on your iPad, including categories from Lifestyle to Travel and Medical.

To use the App Store, you have to first have an Apple ID. This can be obtained when you first connect to the App Store. Once you have an Apple ID you can start exploring the App Store:

Don't forget

For full details about obtaining an Apple ID, see Chapter Five.

1 Tap once on the App Store icon on the Home screen

2 The latest available apps are displayed on the homepage of the App Store, including the iPad App of the Week, featured in the top panel

Don't forget

The Genius function is one that is created within the App Store to highlight similar apps to the ones you have downloaded.

3 Tap on these buttons to view the apps according to Featured, Genius, Top Charts, Categories and Purchased

Viewing apps

To view apps in the App Store and read about their content and functionality:

 Tap once on an app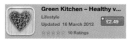

 General details about the app are displayed

Don't forget

If it is an upgraded version of an app, this page will include details of any fixes and improvements that have been made.

3 Swipe left or right here to view additional information about the app and view details from it

4 Ratings and reviews are available at the bottom of the page

Finding Apps

Categories

Within the App Store apps are separated into categories according to type. This enables you to find apps according to particular subjects. To do this:

 Tap once on the Categories button on the toolbar at the bottom of the App Store

 The categories are listed alphabetically

70

Tap once on a category to see the apps within it

Top Chart

To find the top paid for and free apps:

1 Tap once on the Top Charts button on the toolbar at the bottom of the App Store

2 The top overall paid for and free apps are displayed

71

3 To find the top apps in different categories, tap once on this button

4 Tap once on a category

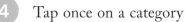

5 The top apps for that category are displayed

...cont'd

Genius

This is a feature which suggests similar apps to those you have already downloaded. To use this:

 Tap once on the Genius button on the toolbar at the bottom of the App Store

 Tap once on the Turn On Genius button

3 Enter your Apple ID details

4 Agree to the Terms and Conditions

5 Tap once on the Done button

6 Relevant recommendations will appear in the Genius window once you have started downloading apps

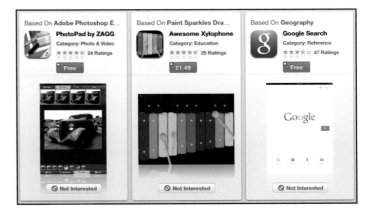

Searching for apps

Another way to find apps is with the App Store Search box, which is located at the top-right corner of the App Store window. To use this:

1 Tap once in the Search box to bring up the iPad virtual keyboard

Don't forget

For more information about using the iPad virtual keyboard see Chapter Three.

2 Enter a search keyword or phrase

3 Suggested apps appear as you are typing

4 Tap once on an app to view it

TripAdvisor City Guides
Travel
Updated 08 March 2012   FREE
☆☆☆☆☆ 13 Ratings

Downloading Apps

When you identify an app that you would like to use, it can be downloaded to your iPad. To do this:

Apps usually download in a few minutes, or less, depending on the speed of your Wi-Fi connection.

 Find the app you want to download and tap once on this button (this will say Free or have a price)

The button changes to say Install App. Tap on this once

Enter your Apple ID details and tap once on the OK button

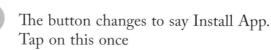

Apple ID Password

nickvandome@mac.com

password

Cancel   OK

Some apps have 'in-app purchases'. This is additional content that has to be paid for when it is downloaded.

The app will begin to download on your iPad

Once the app is downloaded tap once on it to open and use it

Updating Apps

The world of apps is a dynamic and fast-moving one and new apps are being created and added to the App Store on a daily basis. Existing apps are also being updated, to improve their performance and functionality. Once you have installed an app from the App Store it is possible to obtain updates, at no extra cost (if the app was paid for). To do this:

1   When an update is available it is denoted by a red icon on the App Store button, showing how many updates are available

2   Tap once on the App Store button

3   In the App Store, tap once on the Updates button

Hot tip

You should keep your apps as up to date as possible to take advantage of software fixes and any updates to the iPad operating system (iOS).

75

4   The available updates are displayed

iPad 🔋	18:18	Not Charging

Updates   Update All

	iMovie	• Create beautiful movie trailers with stunning graphics and world-class soundtracks* • Swipe up on the playhead to freeze a frame in your video • Preview music and sound effects in the Audio Browser • Create a song in GarageBand and send it directly to iMovie	FREE
	Requires iOS 5.1 or later. 24 June 2010	... More ▼	
	GarageBand	• Start a Jam Session to play or record live with up to three of your friends using iPad, iPhone, or iPod touch* • Conduct an entire string orchestra using Smart Strings • Use the Note Editor to adjust or fine-tune any Touch Instrument recording • Combine recordings to free up additional tracks using Track Merge...	FREE
	Version 1.2 10 March 2011	More ▼	
	Bloomberg for iPad	- Bug fixes for crash that affected app startup after upgrade - My Stocks list remembers the last scroll position instead of reset to the top of the list - Fixed crash while adding to My Stocks...	FREE
	Version 1.1.2 01 April 2010	More ▼	
	Numbers	Numbers 1.6 requires iOS 5.1 software update or later • Create and view stunning 3D bar, line, area, and pie charts • Numbers 1.6 is enhanced to take advantage of the Retina display on the new iPad • Includes performance improvements	FREE
	Requires iOS 5.1 or later. 26 May 2010		

5   Tap once on the button next to an app to update it

6   Tap once on the Update All button to update all of the required apps

Organizing Apps

When you start downloading apps you will probably soon find that you have dozens, if not hundreds, of them. You can move between screens to view all of your apps by swiping left or right with one finger.

As more apps are added it can become hard to find the apps you want, particularly if you have to swipe between several screens. However, it is possible to organize apps into individual folders to make using them more manageable. To do this:

1 Press on an app until it starts to jiggle and a white cross appears at the top-left corner

2 Drag the app over another one

3 A folder is created, containing the two apps

4 The folder is given a default name, usually based on the category of the apps

Beware

Only top-level folders can be created i.e. sub-folders cannot be created within the main one. Also, one folder cannot be placed within another.

5 Tap on the folder name and type a new name if required

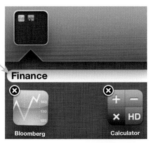

6 Click the Home button once to finish creating the folder

7 Click the Home button again to return to the Home screen (this is done whenever you want to return to the Home screen from an apps folder)

Hot tip

If you want to rename an apps folder after it has been created, tap and hold on it until it starts to jiggle. Then tap on it once and edit the folder name as in Step 5.

8 The folder is added on the Home screen. Tap once on this to access the items within it

Deleting Apps

If you decide that you do not want certain apps anymore, they can be deleted from your iPad. However, they remain in the iCloud so that you can reinstall them if you change your mind. This also means that if you delete an app by mistake you can get it back from the App Store without having to pay for it again. To do this:

1 Press on an app until it starts to jiggle and a white cross appears at the top-left corner

Beware

If you delete an app it will also delete any data that has been compiled with that app, even if you reinstall it from the App Store.

2 Tap once on the white cross to delete the app. In the Delete dialog box, tap once on the Delete button

Don't forget

You cannot delete any of the built-in iPad apps, even by mistake.

3 Tap once on the App Store button

4 Tap once on the Purchased button

5 Apps that have been deleted have this iCloud icon next to them

Pages
Apple
Productivity
Purchased 08 January 2012

6 Tap once on the iCloud button to reinstall an app

78

5 Keeping in Touch

*We live in a world of
varied and instant
communications. This
chapter shows how
to use your iPad to
keep ahead in this fast
moving world.*

Getting Online

iPads can be used for a variety of different communications, but they all require online access. This is done via Wi-Fi and you will need to have an Internet Service Provider and a Wi-Fi router to connect to the Internet. Once this is in place you will be able to connect to a Wi-Fi network:

80

1 Tap once on this icon

Settings

2 Tap once on the Wi-Fi link

Wi-Fi — Not Connected

3 Ensure the Wi-Fi button is in the On position

Wi-Fi — ON

4 Available networks are shown here. Tap once on one to select it

Choose a Network...
NETGEAR
virginmedia6249958
Other...

5 Enter a password for your Wi-Fi router

Enter the password for "NETGEAR"
Cancel — Enter Password — Join
Password ••••••••

6 Tap once on the Join button

7 Once a network has been joined, a tick appears next to it. This now provides access to the Internet

Choose a Network...
✓ NETGEAR

Obtaining an Apple ID

An Apple ID is a registered email address and password with Apple that enables you to login and use a variety of online Apple services. These include:

- App Store
- iTunes Store
- iCloud
- iMessage
- FaceTime
- Games Center
- iBooks

It is free to register for an Apple ID and this can be done when you access one of the apps or services which requires this, or you can do it on the Apple website at My Apple ID:

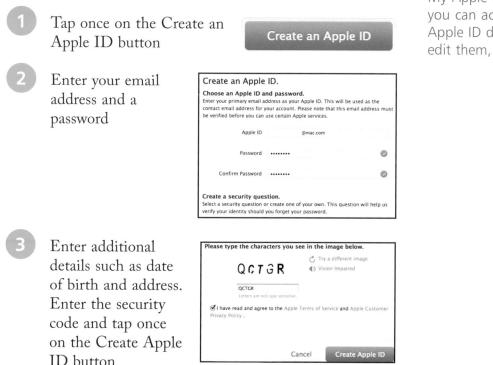

1 Tap once on the Create an Apple ID button

Create an Apple ID

2 Enter your email address and a password

Create an Apple ID.

Choose an Apple ID and password.
Enter your primary email address as your Apple ID. This will be used as the contact email address for your account. Please note that this email address must be verified before you can use certain Apple services.

Apple ID _____ @mac.com

Password ••••••••

Confirm Password ••••••••

Create a security question.
Select a security question or create one of your own. This question will help us verify your identity should you forget your password.

3 Enter additional details such as date of birth and address. Enter the security code and tap once on the Create Apple ID button

Please type the characters you see in the image below.

↻ Try a different image
◀) Vision Impaired

QCTGR

QCTGR
Letters are not case sensitive.

☑ I have read and agree to the Apple Terms of Service and Apple Customer Privacy Policy .

Cancel   **Create Apple ID**

Setting up an Email Account

Email accounts

Email settings can be specified within the Settings app. Different email accounts can also be added here.

1 Tap once on the Settings app

2 Tap once on the Mail, Contacts, Calendars link

Mail, Contacts, Calendars

3 Tap once on the Add Account link to add a new account

Accounts

iCloud
Mail, Contacts, Calendars, Bookmarks, Reminders, Notes, Photo Stream, Documents & Data, Backup >

Add Account... >

4 Tap once on the type of email account you want to add

Add Account...

☁ iCloud

Microsoft Exchange

Gmail

YAHOO!

Hot tip

If your email provider is not on the Add Account list, tap once on Other at the bottom of the list and complete the account details using the information from your email provider.

5 Enter the details for the account. Tap once on the Next button

Cancel	Gmail	Next

Name	Nick Vandome
Address	nickvandome@gmail.com
Password	●●●●●●●●
Description	Gmail

6 Drag these buttons On or Off to determine which items Mail downloads from the required account.

Cancel	Gmail	Save
✉ Mail		ON
📅 Calendars		ON
📓 Notes		OFF

7 Each new account is added under the Accounts heading of the Mail, Contacts, Calendars section

Accounts

iCloud
Mail, Contacts, Calendars, Bookmarks, Reminders, Notes, Photo Stream, Find My iPad and 2 more... ›

Gmail
Mail, Calendars ›

Add Account... ›

Email settings

Email settings can be specified within the Settings app. Different email accounts can also be added here.

1 Under the Mail section there are several options for how Mail operates and looks. These include the number of messages being displayed, previewing emails and font size

Mail

Show	50 Recent Messages ›
Preview	2 Lines ›
Minimum Font Size	Medium ›
Show To/Cc Label	OFF
Ask Before Deleting	OFF
Load Remote Images	ON
Organize By Thread	ON
Always Bcc Myself	OFF
Increase Quote Level	On ›
Signature	Sent from my iPad ›
Default Account	iCloud ›

83

Emailing

Email on the iPad is created, sent and received using the Mail app. This provides a range of functionality for managing email, including adding mailboxes and viewing email conversation threads.

Accessing Mail

To access Mail and start sending and receiving emails:

1 Tap once on this icon (the red icon in the corner displays the number of unread emails in your Inbox)

2 Tap once on a message to display it in the main panel

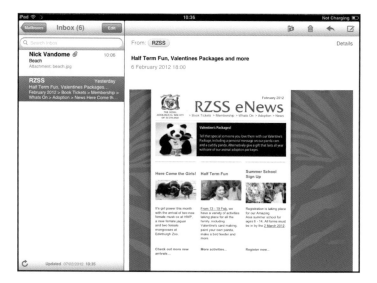

3 Use these buttons to, from left to right, move a message, delete a message, respond to a message and create a new message

4 Tap once on this button to Reply to a message, Forward it to a new recipient, save an image in a message or print it

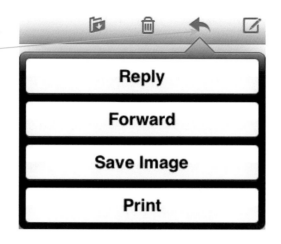

Hot tip

Images in an email can also be saved by tapping and holding on them and then tapping once on the Save Image button.

Creating email

To create and send an email:

1 Tap once on this button to create a new message

2 Enter a recipient name here

To: eilidh

Eildih Vandome
home   eilidhvandome@mac.com

Hot tip

If the recipient is included in your Contacts app, their details will appear as you type. Tap once on the email address, if it appears, to include it in the To field.

3 Enter a subject

Subject: **Lunch tomorrow?**

4 Enter the body text

Subject: Lunch tomorrow?

Hi Eilidh, just wondered if you are around for lunch tomorrow?

Sent from my iPad

5 Tap once on the Send button to send the email to the recipient in Step 2

Send

...cont'd

Mailboxes

Different categories of email messages can be managed via mailboxes. For instance, you may want to keep your social emails separately from ones that apply to financial activities. To use different mailboxes:

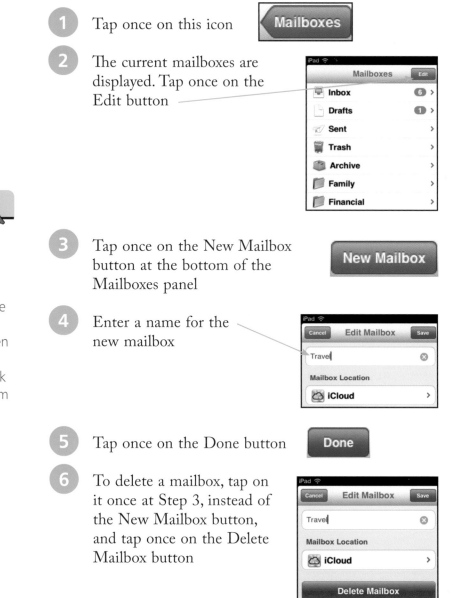

1 Tap once on this icon

2 The current mailboxes are displayed. Tap once on the Edit button

3 Tap once on the New Mailbox button at the bottom of the Mailboxes panel

4 Enter a name for the new mailbox

5 Tap once on the Done button

6 To delete a mailbox, tap on it once at Step 3, instead of the New Mailbox button, and tap once on the Delete Mailbox button

... cont'd

Email threads

When you receive a number of emails on the same subject, as part of a conversation with one or more people, they can be sorted into threads, for easier viewing. To do this:

 1 If there is an email thread, there is a number next to each email

2 Tap once on the email to view the items in the full thread

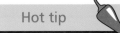

The Threads option can be turned On or Off within Settings>General> Mail, Contacts, Calendars, under the Organize By Thread link in the Mail section.

3 Tap once on an individual email in the thread to view its contents

87

Having a Video Chat

Video chatting is a very personal and interactive way to keep in touch with family and friends around the world. The FaceTime app provides this facility with other iOS 5 users on the iPad, iPhone and iPod Touch, or a Mac computer with FaceTime. To use FaceTime for video chatting:

 Tap once on the FaceTime app

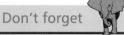
Don't forget

To make video calls with FaceTime you need an active Internet connection.

2 Sign in using your Apple ID to create your FaceTime account

3 Tap once on the Contacts button

4 Tap once on a contact to access their details for making a FaceTime call

5 Tap once on their phone number or email address to make a FaceTime call. The recipient has to have FaceTime on their iPad, iPhone, iPod Touch or Mac computer

6 Tap once on the Add to Favorites button to add the contact to your favorites list, for quick access

7 Once you have selected a contact, FaceTime starts connecting to them and displays this button

8 When you have connected your contact appears in the main window and you appear in a picture-in-picture thumbnail in the corner

Hot tip

The contacts for FaceTime calls are taken from the iPad Contacts app. You can also add new contacts directly to the contacts list by tapping once on the + sign and adding the relevant details for the new contact.

89

9 Tap once on this button to swap between cameras on your iPad

10 Tap once on this button to end the FaceTime call

11 If someone else makes a call to you, tap once on the Decline or Accept buttons

Texting Too

Text messaging should not be thought of as the domain of the younger generation. On your iPad you can join the world of text with the Apple iMessage service that is accessed via the Messages app. This enables text and photo messages to be sent, free of charge, between users of the iOS 5 operating system, on the iPad, iPhone and iPod Touch. iMessages can be sent to mobile/cell phone numbers and email addresses. To use iMessages:

1 Tap once on this icon

2 Enter details for your location and your email address. Tap once on the Next button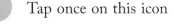

Beware

If a number, or email address, is not recognized it shows up in red in the To box.

3 Tap once on this button to create a new message and start a new conversation

4 Enter a phone number, or email address, here (this has to belong to an iOS 5 user)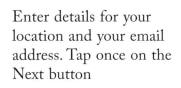

5 Tap once on this button to select someone from your contacts

6 Tap once on a contact to select them as the recipient of the new message

Creating iMessages

To create and edit messages and conversations:

1 Tap once here and type with the keyboard to create a message. Tap once on the Send button

Hi, what are you doing for lunch? | Send

2 As the conversation progresses each message is displayed here

3 Tap once on this button to edit the messages in the current conversation

4 Tap once next to a message and tap once on Delete or Forward at the bottom of the window. Or, tap once on the Clear All button and tap once on the Clear Conversation button to delete the conversation

5 To edit whole conversations, tap once on the Edit button in the Messages panel

Edit

6 Tap once here and tap once on the Delete button to delete the conversation

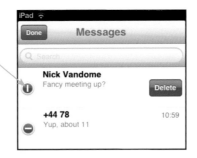

Don't forget

When a message has been sent you are notified underneath it if it has been delivered.

91

Phoning With Skype

Skype is a popular app that is used on computers and mobile devices to make free phone and video calls. To do this, both users have to have Skype installed on their computer or mobile device and have a microphone and speakers attached, either internally or externally.

As well as making free calls to other Skype users, it is also possible to phone standard telephone numbers and, although there is a charge for this, it is frequently cheaper than standard phone charges.

To use Skype:

Downloading Skype

1 Access the App Store and enter Skype in the App Store Search box and tap once on the Skype for iPad link

2 Tap once here on the Skype app to download it

Using Skype
To make calls with Skype:

1 Tap once on the Skype icon

2 To use Skype you are required to register. This requires an email address and password

3 Enter your registration details and tap once on the Sign In button

4 Tap once on this button to search for contacts or add a telephone number of a contact you know

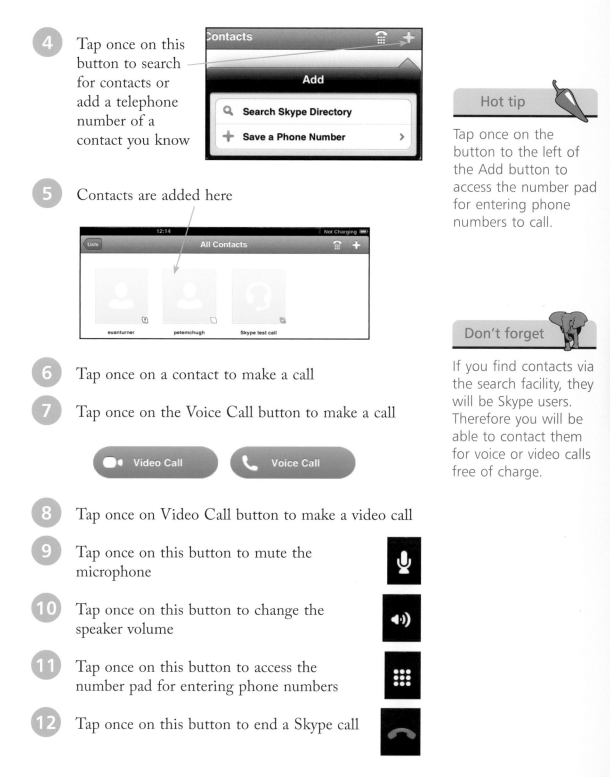

5 Contacts are added here

6 Tap once on a contact to make a call

7 Tap once on the Voice Call button to make a call

8 Tap once on Video Call button to make a video call

9 Tap once on this button to mute the microphone

10 Tap once on this button to change the speaker volume

11 Tap once on this button to access the number pad for entering phone numbers

12 Tap once on this button to end a Skype call

Hot tip

Tap once on the button to the left of the Add button to access the number pad for entering phone numbers to call.

Don't forget

If you find contacts via the search facility, they will be Skype users. Therefore you will be able to contact them for voice or video calls free of charge.

93

Communication Apps

Within the App Store there is a range of communication apps that can be used to contact friends and family via text, phone and video. There are also several apps for sharing information, updates and photos. Some of these are:

- Facebook. The social networking phenomenon, that has millions of users around the world. This app enables you to create and use a Facebook account from your iPad. You can then interact with friends and family around the world by posting messages, comments and photos

- Twitter. Another of the top social networking sites on the Web. It provides the facility to post text messages of up to 140 characters. You can choose other users to follow, so you see their messages (tweets) and other people can follow you too

- Flickr. An iPad version of the popular photo and video sharing site. You have to register and once you have done this you can share your photos and videos with a vast online community

- Pictures with Words. Another photo sharing app that enables you to share your photos online and also add captions, text and graphics to your images

- Wordpress. A web publishing app that can be used to create online blogs and also your own websites

- Gmail. If you have a Gmail account this will enable you to access it directly from your iPad

- Windows Live Hotmail. This can be used to access email from a Hotmail (or MSN or Live) account

- Yahoo! Messenger. This app is similar to Skype in that it offers free video and voice calling to other Yahoo! Messenger users

- Talkatone for Google Voice and Facebook. Another app for free phone calls and texts to phones in the USA and Canada

Hot tip

On Facebook you can have private text conversations with your friends, as well as posting public information for all of your contacts to see.

Beware

When you follow people on Twitter, their tweets appear on your homepage. If they are very prolific, or you follow a lot of people, this may result in a lot of messages to read.

6 On a Web Safari

No computer experience is complete without access to the Web. This chapter shows how to use the iPad Web browser, Safari, to enjoy the online world.

Around Safari

The Safari app is the default Web browser on the iPad. This can be used to view Web pages, save favorites and read pages with the Reader function. To start using Safari:

 Tap once on this icon

 Tap once on the Address Bar at the top of the Safari window. Type a Web page address

 Tap once on the Go button on the keyboard to open the Web page

 Also, suggested options appear as you type. Tap once on one of these to go to this page

 The selected Web page opens in Safari

96

6 The selected Web page opens in Safari. Swipe up and down and left and right to navigate around the page

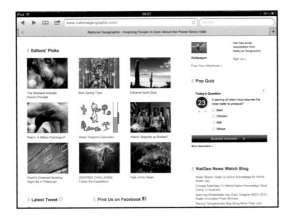

7 Swipe outwards with thumb and forefinger to zoom in on a Web page (pinch inwards to zoom back in)

97

Safari Settings

Settings for Safari can be specified in the Settings app. To do this:

1 Tap once on the Settings app

2 Tap once on the Safari link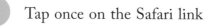

3 Tap once on the Search Engine link to select a default search engine to use

General	
Search Engine	Google >

4 Tap once on the default search engine you want to use with Safari

Google	✓
Yahoo!	
Bing	

5 Tap once here for options for filling in online forms

AutoFill	Names and Passwords >

6 Drag this button to On to open new pages in the background of your current page

Open New Tabs in Background	ON

7 Drag this button to On to keep the Bookmarks Bar in view under the Address Bar in Safari

Always Show Bookmarks Bar	ON

Beware

Don't use Autofill for names and passwords for any sites with sensitive information, such as banking sites, if other people have access to the iPad.

Hot tip

If the Open New Tabs in Background is set to On, you can tap and hold on a link on a Web page and select Open in New Tab. The link then opens in a new tab behind the one you are viewing so as not to interrupt what you are doing.

...cont'd

8 Drag the Private Browsing button to Off to disable this. If Private Browsing is On then no information will be recorded about visited websites

Privacy	
Private Browsing	◯ OFF
Accept Cookies	From visited ❯

9 Tap once on the Accept Cookies link to specify how Safari deals with cookies from websites

10 Tap once on Clear History and Clear Cookies and Data to remove these items

Clear History
Clear Cookies and Data

11 Drag this button to On to enable alerts for when you have visited a fraudulent website

Security	
Fraud Warning	ON ◯

12 Drag these buttons to On to enable Javascript files on websites and also block pop-up messages

JavaScript	ON ◯
Block Pop-ups	ON ◯

Don't forget

Cookies are small items from websites that obtain details from your browser when you visit a site. The cookie remembers the details for the next time you visit the site.

Beware

If the History is cleared then there will be no record of any sites that have been visited.

Don't forget

Javascript files provide additional functionality for some websites.

66

Navigating Pages

When you are viewing pages within Safari there are a number of functions that can be used:

1 Tap once on these buttons to move forward and back between Web pages that have been visited

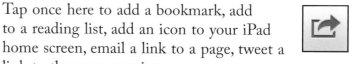

2 Tap once here to view bookmarked pages and also Reading List pages

3 Tap once here to add a bookmark, add to a reading list, add an icon to your iPad home screen, email a link to a page, tweet a link to the page or print a page

4 Enter a keyword here to search for a topic

Google

5 Tap once on a link on a page to open it. Tap and hold to access additional options, to open in a new tab, add to a Reading List or copy the link

http://www.nationalgeographic.com/news/2012/03/120320-recta...baru-space-science/

Open

Open in New Tab

Add to Reading List

Copy

Small Areas
• Weird Rectangular Galaxy Found

6 Tap and hold on an image and tap once on Save Image or Copy

Save Image

Copy

Opening New Tabs

Safari supports tabbed browsing, which means that you can open separate pages within the same window and access them by tapping on their tab at the top of the page:

 Tap once here to open a new tab for another page

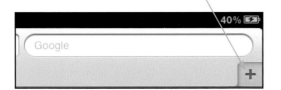

 The page is opened in the new tab

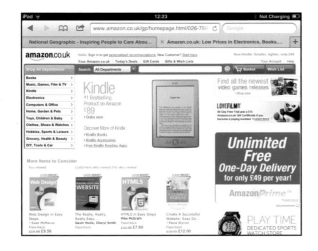

Don't forget

A maximum of nine tabbed pages can be used at the same time within Safari.

 Tap once on the tab headings to move between tabbed pages

 Tap once on the cross at the top of a tab to close it

Bookmarking Pages

Once you start using Safari you will soon build up a collection of favorite pages that you visit regularly. To access these quickly they can be bookmarked so that you can then go to them in one tap. To set up bookmarks:

1 Open a Web page that you want to bookmark. Tap once here and tap once on the Add Bookmark link

2 Tap once on this link and select whether to include the bookmark on the Bookmarks Bar or in a Bookmarks folder

3 Tap once on the Save button

4 Tap once here to view all of the items on the Bookmarks Bar, if they do not fit along the top of the screen

5 Tap once here and tap once on the Bookmarks button to view all of the bookmarks

6 The Bookmarks folders are listed. Tap once on the Edit button to delete or rename the folders

Don't forget

The Bookmarks Bar appears underneath the Address Bar in Safari.

102

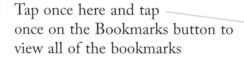

Safari Reader

The Safari Reader is a function that can be used to read individual items on a Web page without having any other of the content as a distraction:

1 In the Address Bar, if the Reader button appears it means that this function is available

2 Tap once on the Reader button to view the page in this format

3 Rotate the screen to portrait to enable the text to fill more of the screen

4 Tap once on the Reader button again to return to the standard page format

Don't forget

Not all Web pages have the Reader function. If the Reader button in Step 1 is not visible in the Address Bar then there is not a Reader function.

Hot tip

The text on the Reader page can be increased in size by tapping once on this icon at the top left-hand corner of the Reader page.

Web Apps

Although Safari can comfortably fulfill all of your Web browsing needs, there are a number of other browser apps that can be downloaded from the App Store. A lot of these have a free (lite) version and there is sometimes a small charge for the full version. Generally, they have similar functionality but each has its own features too. It is worth looking at a few to compare the different interfaces. Some to try are:

- Atomic Web Browser. This is a browser that has a full-screen view, one-touch tabbed browsing and also a wider range of Multi-Touch Gestures for navigating around

- Dolphin Browser. This browser has four different search engines from which to choose and Gestures and Sidebars for quickly accessing pages

- Mercury Web Browser. A stylish browser which includes customizable themes, ten tab browsing, full screen view and effective download option for links or images

- Opera Mini Web Browser. This is a fast browser that compresses data before downloading it for viewing. One of the fastest browsers available for the iPad

Beware

Flash is a video and animation format that is used widely on the Web. However, Flash video files cannot usually be played on the iPad.

- SkyFire Web Browser. This is an iPad browser with the unique feature of being able to play Flash video files. It does this by processing the content on their own servers and then sending it back to the browser. It is invaluable if you want to watch a lot of Flash video.

7 Staying Organized

An iPad is ideal for all of your organization needs. This chapter shows how to use address books and calendars, keep notes and set reminders. It also details productivity apps for creating documents.

Making Notes

It is always useful to have a quick way of making notes of everyday things, such as shopping lists, recipes or packing lists for travelling. On your iPad the Notes app is perfect for this function. To use it:

1 Tap once on this icon

2 Tap once on the note to access the keyboard. Start writing the note

3 Tap once on this button on the keyboard to hide the keyboard and finish the note. To edit an existing note, tap once on the text and the keyboard will reappear

4 As the note is created it appears in the Notes panel. The most recent note is at the top and the first line of the note is the title. Tap once on a note to view it

Accounts	3 Notes	
Q Search		
My Packing List		17:51
My Shopping List		17:51
My To Do List		17:42

Sending notes to iCloud

If you are using iCloud this can be used to send your notes to your iCloud email address. To do this:

1 Access the Settings app and tap once on the iCloud link

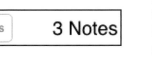

2 Drag the Notes button to On

3 In the Notes app, tap once on the Accounts button to view your iPad and iCloud notes

4 Tap on the links to view the notes in those categories

Accounts	
All Notes	>
On My iPad	>
iCloud	>

If iCloud is set up for Notes then all of your notes will appear in the iCloud account. If not they will all appear in the On My iPad account. Once in a specific account each note stays there, where it was created.

107

Setting Reminders

Another useful organization app is Reminders. This enables you to create lists for different topics and then set reminders for specific items. A date and time can be set for each reminder and, when this is reached, the reminder appears on your iPad screen. To use Reminders:

1 Tap once on this icon

2 The Reminder lists are located in the left-hand panel. Tap once on a list name

Hot tip

For a recurring reminder, tap once on the Repeat link at Step 5 and select a repeat option from None, Every Day, Every Week, Every 2 Weeks, Every Month, Every Year. The reminder will then appear at the specified timescale, at the time set in Step 7.

3 Tap once on a new line and enter the reminder

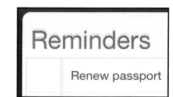

4 Hide the keyboard and tap once on the reminder to access the details window

5 Tap once on the Remind Me link to set a day and time for the reminder

6   Drag this button to On

7   Tap once on the date and select a time and date for when you want the reminder alert

Don't forget

Set the time and date for reminders by dragging up and down on the relevant barrels within the Remind Me window. The time can be set in five minute intervals.

8   Tap once on the Done button 

9   At the date and time of the reminder, a popup box appears

10   Tap once on the View button to see the details of the reminder

...cont'd

Editing Reminders
To edit the way reminders appear:

1 Tap once on the Date button to view reminders according to the dates on which they have been set

2 Tap once on the Edit button

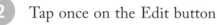

3 Tap once on the Create New List link to create a new reminders list

4 Tap once on the red circle next to a list and tap once on the Delete button to delete it

5 Tap once on the Done button

6 Within a list, tap once on this button to create a new reminder item

7 Tap once on this box next to a reminder to put it in the Completed list

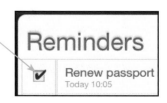

Your iPad Address Book

There is a built-in address book app on your iPad: Contacts. This enables you to store contact details which can then be used to contact people, via email, iMessages or FaceTime. To add contacts:

1 Tap once on this icon

2 Tap once on this button to add a new contact **+**

3 Enter the required details for a contact

4 Tap once on the Done button

Done

Cancel   Info   Done

add photo   Lucy

Vandome

Company

iPhone   07989 987654

mobile   Phone

home   lucyvandome@gmail.com

5 Tap once on a contact to select them

6 Use these buttons to contact via text message (iMessage), video chat (FaceTime), share their contact details or add to your favorite contacts

Send Message   FaceTime

Share Contact   Add to Favorites

Edit

7 Tap once on the Edit button to edit details about an individual entry

Edit

8 To delete a contact swipe to the bottom of the window in Edit mode and tap once on the Delete Contact button

Delete Contact

Hot tip

Tap once on a contact's email address to go directly to Mail to send them an email. Tap once on a mobile/cell phone number to access FaceTime for a video call (if the recipient is set up for this).

111

Don't forget

Contact details of an individual can be shared via email or as an iMessage.

Using the Calendar

The built-in iPad Calendar can be used to create and view appointments and events. To do this:

112

1 Tap once on this icon

2 By default the calendar is displayed in a single day view, opening at the current day

3 Tap once here to view the calendar by Week, Month, Year or List view. Swipe left or right to move between days, weeks, months or years

4 Tap once on the Today button to view the current date. Tap once on the bar to move between dates

5 Tap once on this button to create a new event

6 Enter a Title and a Location for the event

7 Tap once on the Ends link to set a timescale for the event

...cont'd

8   Drag on the barrels here to set an end time for the event. Tap once on the Done button

Don't forget

Drag the All-day button to On to set the event for the whole day.

9   To invite other people to the event, tap once on the Invitees link (these will be people who you can select from your Contacts)

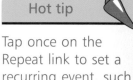
Hot tip

Tap once on the Repeat link to set a recurring event, such as a birthday. The repeat options are Every Day, Every Week, Every 2 Weeks, Every Month or Every Year.

10   Tap once on this button

11   Tap once on a contact to select them

12   Tap once on the Done button. An email invitation will then be sent to the recipient's email address

113

Keeping Notified

Although the Notification Center feature is not an app in its own right, it can be used to display information from a variety of apps. These appear as a list for all of the items you want to be reminded about or be made aware of. Notifications are set up within the Settings app. To do this:

1 Tap once on this icon

2 Tap once on the Notifications link

3 The apps included in the Notification Center are listed here. Tap once on an app to edit its Notification Center settings

In Notification Center	
FaceTime Badges, Alerts	>
Messages Badges, Banners	>
Reminders Alerts	>
Calendar Badges, Alerts	>

Don't forget

Tap once on an item in the Notification Center to view that item in its specific app.

4 Drag this button On or Off to specify whether the selected item appears in the Notification Center

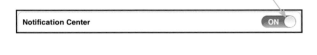

Notification Center ON

5 Drag downwards from the top of the screen to view the Notification Center

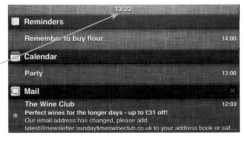

Organization Apps

In the App Store there is a wide range of organization apps for tasks such as notetaking. Some of these are:

- Evernote. One of the most popular note-taking apps. You can create individual notes and also save them into notebook folders. Evernote works across multiple devices so, if it is installed on other computers or mobile devices, you can access your notes wherever you are

- Popplet. This is an innovative note-taking app that enables you to link notes together, so you can form a mindmap type creation. You can also include photos and draw pictures

- Dropbox. This is an online service for storing and accessing files. You can upload files from your iPad and then access them from other devices with an Internet connection

- Bamboo Paper. This is another note-taking app, but it allows you to do this by handwriting rather than typing. The free version comes with one notebook into which you can put your notes and the paid-for version provides another 20

- Errands To-Do List. A virtual To-Do list that can help keep you organized and up to date. You can create your own folders for different items and have alerts remind you of important dates, events and items

- Notability. Another app that utilizes handwriting for creating notes. It also accommodates word processing, and audio recording

- Alarmed. An app for keeping you on time and up to date. It has an alarm clock, pop-up reminders and pop-up timers

- Grocery List. Shopping need never be the same again with this virtual shopping list app

- World Calendar. Find out public holiday information for 40 countries around the world

Don't forget

Most organization apps are found in the Productivity category of the App Store.

Beware

For handwriting to work most effectively in Bamboo Paper, Multi-Touch Gestures should be turned Off in the Settings app.

Productivity Apps

If you want to do more than just use organization apps, there are some excellent productivity apps for creating word processing documents, presentations and spreadsheets. These can be used to write letters, produce holiday presentations or do household accounts. Some of the productivity apps are:

- Pages. This is a powerful word processing app that has been developed by Apple. It can be used to create and save documents which can then be printed or shared via email or copied to iTunes. There are a number of templates on which documents can be based. There is also a range of formatting and content options so it is possible to create engaging and eye-catching documents

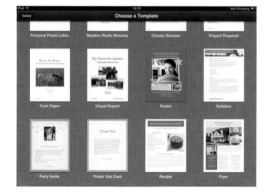

- Keynote. Another Apple productivity app, this is a presentation app that can be used to create slides that can then be played as a presentation

- Numbers. This is the spreadsheet app that is part of the same suite as Pages and Keynote. Again, templates are provided or you can create your spreadsheets from scratch to keep track of expenditure or household bills. You can enter formula into cells to perform simple, or complicated, calculations

- Smart Office 2. This app can be used to create, edit and share Microsoft Office documents, such as Word, Powerpoint and Excel. It supports all Microsoft Office versions since 1997 and also allows viewing of a variety of image files and PDF files

- iA Writer. A simple but effective word processing app. It creates documents that can be synchronized across other devices and also copied to iCloud or Dropbox

- Free Spreadsheet. This is similar to Numbers and although it does not have the same range of functionality it is still an effective spreadsheet

- GoodReader for iPad. This is an app for viewing PDF documents and large documents such as manuals or long books. It also has a facility for annotating PDF documents with text boxes, notes and drawings

Don't forget

PDF stands for Portable Document Format which is a file format created by Adobe to enable documents to be shared across different platforms without losing their formatting.

Saving Documents

For anyone who has grown up with computers and is used to a clear file structure, the first question when faced with an iPad is sometimes, 'Where do I save things?'. Unlike a Windows PC with Windows Explorer, or a Mac with the Finder, there is no obvious place to save files or create folders for content. This is because there isn't one. So where do you save your letters, presentations or photos once they have been created?

Self-contained saving

Instead of having a separate structure into which you can save files, content is saved within the apps in which they are created. So if you write a letter with the Pages word processing app, this is where is will be saved, and similarly if you create a note within the Notes app. Documents can be viewed as follows: (this is for Pages)

Hot tip

iPad apps save content automatically as it is being created so you do not have to remember to keep saving it as you work.

1 Tap once on the Documents button

2 All saved documents can be viewed here

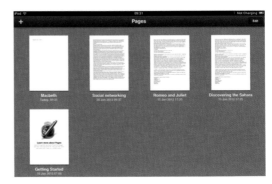

3 When new documents are created they are added to this section. This is essentially the top level folder

Adding folders

Despite the lack of a folder structure within the iPad operating system, folders can be created within some productivity apps, such as Pages. To do this:

1 Tap and hold on a document until it starts to jiggle. Drag it over another document icon

2 The new folder is created. Tap once here to give it a relevant name, then tap anywhere outside the folder to finish, or tap once on Done on the keyboard

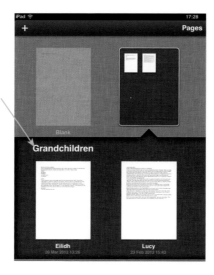

Beware

You cannot create sub-folders, i.e. folders within folders. So the folder structure can only go down one level and you cannot copy one folder into another one.

3 The new folder appears in the main document area next to existing files

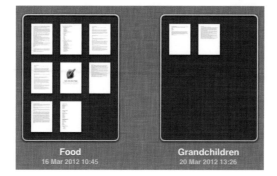

Printing Items

Printing from an iPad has advantages and disadvantages. The advantage is that it is done wirelessly so you do not have to worry about connecting wires and cables to a printer. The disadvantage is that there are a limited number of printers that work with the iPad printing system.

AirPrint

Content from an iPad is printed using the AirPrint system that is part of the iOS 5 operating system. This is a wireless printing system that connects to your printer through your Wi-Fi network. However, there are a limited number of printers that are AirPrint enabled so it may not work with your current printer.

AirPrint can print content from Safari, Mail, Photos, Pages, Keynote, Numbers and PDF documents in iBooks. Some third-party apps have AirPrint facilities but this depends on individual developers. To print items using AirPrint:

Don't forget

Check on the Apple website for a list of AirPrint-enabled printers.

Beware

Some developers offer third-party printing apps for the iPad. However, these work with varying degrees of success.

1. Tap once on the tools option and select one of the Print options

2. Tap once on the Print link

3. Select a printer or, if it has already been setup, tap once on the Print button to print

4. If your printer is not AirPrint compatible this will be shown in the Printer dialog box

8 Just Like a Good Book

This chapter looks at reading material on your iPad.

Newspapers and Magazines

With its portability and high-resolution Retina screen, the iPad is ideal for reading material, from magazines and newspapers to books. The former can be downloaded and read with the Newsstand app and the latter with the iBooks app. To access reading material with the Newsstand:

1 Tap once on this icon

Don't forget

There is a wide range of newspapers available through the Newsstand, usually specific to your geographical location.

122

2 The Newsstand bookcase is initially empty. Tap once on the Store button to access the Newsstand store

3 The Newsstand Store is incorporated within the App Store. Items can be found in the main featured panel or by swiping left and right between items underneath the top panel

Beware

The majority of magazines and newspapers are initially free to download. However, most then require a paid-for subscription once the initial trial period for the item has expired.

4 When you have found a suitable magazine, newspaper or journal, review and download it in the same way as with an app in the App Store

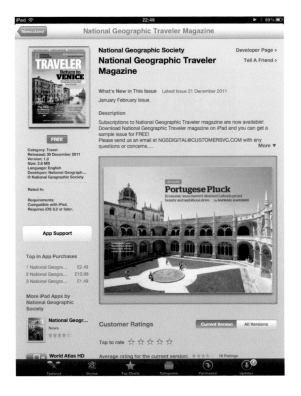

5 Downloaded items appear on the Newsstand bookcase (Library). Tap once on a cover to open that publication

Hot tip

If there is a red circle with a number in it on the Newsstand app, this indicates available updates for your existing publications.

123

...cont'd

Reading magazines and newspapers
Once you have downloaded a publication you can then start browsing through it. To do this:

 1 Tap once on an item on the cover to view it

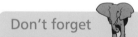
2 Tap once on a page to access the top toolbar

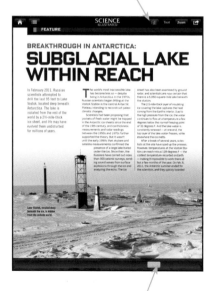

 3 Drag on this bar to move through the publication

4 Tap once on this button to view the publication's homepage

5 Tap once on this button to view the content of the current edition including cover page, table of contents and features

6 Tap once on this button to zoom in on a page. Tap once again to return to standard view

Hot tip

Pages can also be zoomed in on by using the Multi-Touch Gesture of swiping outwards with thumb and forefinger.
To zoom back in, pinch inwards with thumb and forefinger.

7 Tap once on this button to share a page via email, to Facebook or to your Photo Album in the Photos app

Finding Books

For anyone interested in reading, the iPad removes the need to carry around a lot of bulky books. If you are in the home, or traveling, you can keep hundreds of books on your iPad. This is done with the iBooks app, which can be used to download and read books across most genres: it is your own library in your pocket. To use iBooks:

1. Access the iBooks app in the App Store and download it in the same way as any other app

2. Tap once on this icon once the iBooks app has been downloaded

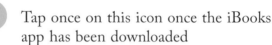

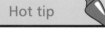
3. The iBooks app interface consists of a bookcase, which initially is empty. Tap once on the Store button to access the iBooks store

4. Navigate through the iBooks Store in the same way as the App Store to find the required titles

5. Use these buttons to search for items within the iBooks Store (see next two pages)

Looking for books

The buttons at the bottom of the iBooks window can be used to look for books in different ways:

1 Tap once on this button to view the top selling books, for both paid-for and free books

2 Tap once on this button to view different categories of books. Tap once on a category to view all of the books within it

...cont'd

3 Tap once on this button to look for books by author. Tap once on an author's name to see their available titles and editions

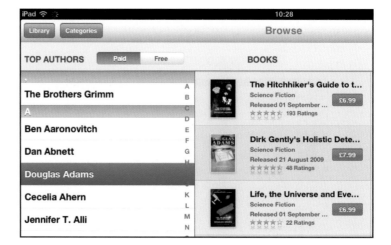

4 Tap once on this button to view the books that you have already downloaded or bought

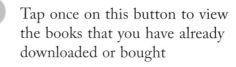

Downloading books

Once you have identified appropriate books they can then be downloaded to the iBooks bookcase (library). To do this:

 Tap once on the book name or title to view its details

2 Review the details of the book and any reviews that have been written about it

Don't forget

On the Review page there are usually details of other books that people have bought, in addition to the one being viewed.

129

3 Tap once on this button to download a sample of the book

GET SAMPLE

4 Tap once here to download the book

£3.99

5 Downloaded books appear on the iBooks bookcase. Tap once on a book cover to open it and start reading

Reading Books

Reading an iBook

Once you have opened an iBook there are a number of ways to navigate around and work with the content:

Hot tip

To hide the toolbar, tap once on a page.

Don't forget

From the Table of Contents, tap once on the Resume button to return to the page you where looking at.

Don't forget

If you are viewing a sample version of a book, there is a Buy button on the top toolbar. Tap once on this to buy the full version of the book.

1 Tap once in the middle of a page in an iBook to access the top toolbar

2 Tap once on this button to return to the iBook Library (bookcase)

3 Tap once on this button to view the Table of Contents

4 Tap once on this button to change the text size

5 Tap once on this button to search for an item in the book

6 Tap once on this button to bookmark a page

7 Drag on this bottom bar to move through the book

Working with text

When you are reading an iBook there are a number of options for enhancing the reading experience, from looking up dictionary definitions of words, to making notes about the text. To do this:

1 Tap and hold on a word to highlight it and access the text toolbar

2 Tap once on the Define button to access a dictionary definition for the selected word. At the bottom of the window there are also options for searching the word over the Web or Wikipedia

Beware

If you use the Search Web or Search Wikipedia option, this takes you away from the iBook page.

131

3 Highlight a word and drag on the blue dots to extend the highlighted area

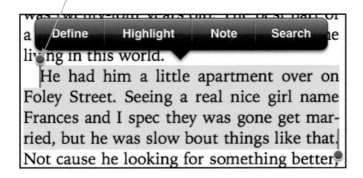

...cont'd

4 Tap once on the Highlight button and select an option for how the text is highlighted

Highlight

> was twenty-four years old. The best part of
> living in this world.
> He had him a little apartment over on Foley Street. Seeing a real nice girl name Frances and I spec they was gone get married, but he was slow bout things like that.

Beware

The more words you highlight for a search, the fewer results will be returned.

132

5 Highlight a word and tap once on the Search button

> le Mobley my special baby
> | Define | Highlight | Note | Search |
> WN BOY, Treelore, ght be-
> waiting on Miss Leefolt. He
> ur years old. The best part of

6 The Search results show where the highlight word appears in the book. Tap one of the instances to go to that section in the book

> **The Help**   ᴀA Q 🔖
>
> Q Leefolt   ✕
>
> **Text**
>
> **THE HELP, Page 11**
> But I ain't never seen a baby yell like Mae Mobley **Leefolt**.
>
> **THE HELP, Page 12**
> Miss **Leefolt**, she look terrified a her own child.
>
> **THE HELP, Page 12**
> But Miss **Leefolt**, she don't pick up her own baby for the rest a the day.

7 Highlight a word or phrase and tap once on the Note button

> even look out the window, s e if the world
> st   Define   Highlight   Note   Search   d
> di n't stop just cause my boy did.
>   Five months after the funeral, I lifted
> myself up out a bed. I put on my white
> uniform and put my little gold cross back

8 Enter your own note for the selected item

> was dead.
>   T   When did this happen?   ent
> bla   laid
> up   s a
> my   ake
> sur   i to
> kee   re I
> eve   orld
> still   orld
> didn't just cause my boy did.
>   Five months after the funeral, I lifted
> myself up out a bed. I put on my white

Don't forget

When Notes are created they are highlighted in the same way as a standard highlighted piece of text. However, there is a yellow notes icon in the margin to identify it as a note.

133

9 On the Table of Contents page, tap once on the Bookmarks button to view all of the bookmarked pages. Tap once on an item to view it

> CONTENTS   **BOOKMARKS**   NOTES
>
> THE HELP   12
>   Today

10 On the Table of Contents page, tap once on the Notes button to view all of the notes you have made in the book

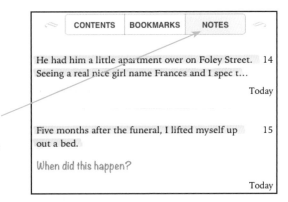

> CONTENTS   BOOKMARKS   **NOTES**
>
> He had him a little apartment over on Foley Street. 14
> Seeing a real nice girl name Frances and I spec t...
>   Today
>
> Five months after the funeral, I lifted myself up 15
> out a bed.
>
> When did this happen?
>   Today

Kindle on Your iPad

The Kindle is the most popular eReader device for reading eBooks. However, it is now possible to use the Kindle app on your iPad. If you already have a Kindle account, on Amazon, then you can also import books that you have downloaded to your iPad. To use Kindle on your iPad:

1 Download the Kindle app from the Books category in the App Store

2 Tap once on this icon to open the Kindle app

3 If you have a Kindle account, enter the details here to register your iPad Kindle. Tap once on the Register this Kindle button

4 Tap once on this button to view the titles that are in the Kindle Cloud i.e. have been downloaded to your Kindle account on Amazon

Don't forget

When you first access the Kindle on your iPad you will be asked if you want to access titles that you have previously downloaded to your Kindle. After this they will appear in the Cloud section.

5 Tap once on this button to download a title from the Cloud to your iPad

6 Tap once on the Device button to view items that have been downloaded to your iPad

Beware

If you download a book from the Kindle Cloud it only appears under the Device button and not in your iBooks app.

135

7 Tap once on this button to view your books in list or icon view

8 Tap once on this button to sort your books by Most Recent, Title or Author

9 Tap once on this button to access Settings and other options for your Kindle on your iPad

Info
Settings >
Send-to-Kindle E-mail Address nickvandome_74@kindle.com
About >
Provide Feedback >
Contact Support >
Terms of Use >
Legal Notices >

...cont'd

Reading on the Kindle app

When you are reading a book on the Kindle app there are similar options for navigating around as reading an iBook:

1 Tap once on this button to return to the main Library homepage

2 Tap once in the top right-hand corner of a page to add a bookmark

3 Tap once on these buttons to, from left to right, move to the previous page, search for an item in a book and view options for moving to various parts of the book such as table of contents and bookmarks

52%   Page 199 of 370   Location 3469 of 6715

Don't forget

Tap once in the middle of a page to show or hide the toolbars.

4 Drag on this button to move through the book

5 Tap once on this button on the bottom toolbar to view options for the way the page is displayed. This includes text size and options for viewing black on white, white on black or sepia tone paper effect

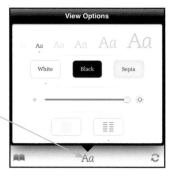

6 If you are also reading books on a Kindle, tap once on this button on the bottom toolbar to synchronize your iPad version of the book with the Kindle one

9 Enjoying Leisure Time

The possibilities for enjoying yourself with your iPad are huge. This chapter looks at downloading and listening to music and capturing and using photos and videos in different creative ways. It also covers some lifestyle opportunities and shows how you can obtain apps for viewing art, drawing, health, cookery and playing popular games.

Buying Music

Music on the iPad can be downloaded and played using the iTunes and the Music apps respectively. iTunes links to the iTunes Store, from where music, and other content, can be bought and downloaded to your iPad. To do this:

You need to have an Apple ID with credit or debit card details added to be able to buy music from the iTunes Store.

Don't forget

If you have iTunes on another computer you can synchronize your music (and other items) that you have there to your iPad. To do this, attach the iPad to your computer (with the Dock Connector to USB Cable) and follow the setup instructions via iTunes. You can check off the Automatically Sync options so that you can choose which items to sync to your iPad. This can ensure too much content is not downloaded to your iPad. To manually update items, drag them from your iTunes Library over the iPad icon under Devices.

1   Tap once on this icon

2   Tap once on the Music button on the iTunes toolbar at the bottom of the window

3   Use these buttons at the top of the window to find music

4   Tap once on an item to view it. Tap once here to buy an album or tap on the button next to a song to buy that individual item

5   Purchased items are included in the Music app's Library

Playing Music

Once music has been bought on iTunes it can be played on your iPad using the Music app. To do this:

 Tap once on this icon

 Use these buttons to find songs by different criteria

 Tap once on a track to select it and start it playing

Hot tip

To create a Playlist of songs, tap once on the Playlist button, then tap once on the New button. Give it a name and then add songs from your Library.

139

4 Tap once on the middle button to pause/play a selected song

5 Drag this button to increase or decrease the volume

6 Tap once on this button to repeat a song or album after it has played

7 Tap once on this button to shuffle the order of songs

Hot tip

Music controls, including Play, Fast Forward, Rewind and Volume can be accessed by double-clicking the Home button on the iPad and swiping left to right on the Multitasking Bar.

Taking Photos

Because of its mobility and the quality of the Retina screen, the iPad is excellent for taking and displaying photos. Photos can be captured directly using one of the two built-in cameras (one on the front and one on the back) and then viewed, edited and shared using the Photos app. To do this:

Don't forget

The front camera on the iPad is an iSight 5 megapixel device. This is capable of capturing high quality images and also HD videos.

1 Tap once on the Camera app

2 Tap once on this button to capture a photo

3 Tap once on this button to swap between the front or back cameras on the iPad

4 Tap once on the Options button

5 Drag the Grid button to On to place a grid over the screen, if required. This can make it easier to frame photos by positioning items according to the lines in the grid

Beware

Be careful to keep your fingers away from the camera lens when you are taking photos, particularly when you are using the camera on the other side of the iPad.

Viewing Photos

Once photos have been captured they can be viewed and organized in the Photos app. To do this:

 Tap once on the Photos app

 All photos, and videos, that have been taken are shown here, under the Photos section

3 Tap once on a photo to view it at full screen size

4 Swipe with one finger or drag here to move through all of the available photos

5 Tap once with two fingers to return the photo to its thumbnail size, or tap once on the Photos button

Hot tip

If you have iCloud set up, all of your photos will also be saved under the Photo Stream button. This enables all of your photos to be made available on any other devices you have with iCloud, such as an iPhone, an iPod Touch or a Mac computer.

Don't forget

To delete photos from the Photos section, tap once on this button, tap once on an item to select it and tap once on the Delete button.

Working With Photos

Creating a slideshow

Photos can also be viewed in a slideshow format in the Photos app. To do this:

1 Tap once on the Slideshow button, either in the Photos section or when a photo is being viewed at full screen size

2 Tap once on the Transitions link to select the way photos move between each other. Drag the Play Music button On or Off to select whether music is played. Tap once on the Start Slideshow button

Sharing photos

Within the Photos app there are a number of ways to share and use photos. To do this:

1 Open a photo at full size and tap once on this button

2 Tap once on one of the options for sharing the photo. These include emailing, adding to a contact in your Contacts app, using as your iPad wallpaper, tweeting, printing and copying the photo

Editing photos

The Photos app has options to perform some basic photo editing operations. To do this:

1️⃣ Open a photo at full screen size and tap once on the Edit button

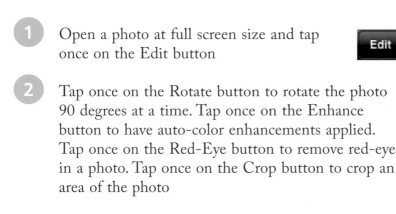

2️⃣ Tap once on the Rotate button to rotate the photo 90 degrees at a time. Tap once on the Enhance button to have auto-color enhancements applied. Tap once on the Red-Eye button to remove red-eye in a photo. Tap once on the Crop button to crop an area of the photo

Creating albums

Within the Photo app it is possible to create different albums into which you can store photos. To do this:

1️⃣ Tap once on the Albums button

2️⃣ Tap once on the Edit button

3️⃣ Tap once on the New Album button

4️⃣ Enter a name for the new album

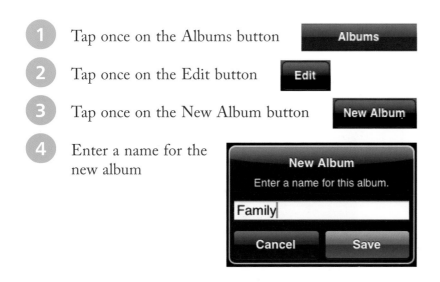

5️⃣ Tap once on the Save button

Don't forget

To add items to an album, tap once on this button in the Photos section.
Tap once on photos to select them, then tap once on the Add To button and select either the Add to Existing Album or Add to New Album option.

In the Photo Booth

The Photo Booth app is one of the built-in iPad apps that can be used to create fun, creative photo effects. To use it:

 Tap once on this icon

 The different special effects are shown through the camera. Tap once to select the desired effect

 Check the image and capture it by tapping once on the camera button

Creating a Picture Frame

The iPad is such a thing of beauty that there is no reason why you should not make use of it even when you are not using it. The Picture Frame option enables you to display photos on the Retina screen when it is not in use:

1 Tap once on the Settings app

2 Tap once on the Picture Frame link

3 Select the settings for your Picture Frame

Picture Frame	
Picture Frame mode turns your iPad into an animated picture frame.	
Transition	
Dissolve	✓
Origami	
Show Each Photo For	3 Seconds >
Zoom in on Faces	ON
Shuffle	ON
All Photos	✓
Albums	

4 When your iPad is locked, tap once on this button

5 Your photos are displayed according to the settings in Step 3

Don't forget

The Picture Frame has to be activated each time that the screen is locked, by tapping once on the button in Step 4.

Capturing Videos

The iPad cameras can also be used to capture video, as well as photos. To do this:

 Tap once on the Camera app

Drag this button to the right so that it is underneath the video camera icon

Tap once on this button to swap cameras from front to back

Tap once on this button to record a video. Tap once on it again to stop recording

Once a video has been captured it is saved within the Photos app with the video camera icon and the duration of the video showing on the thumbnail. Tap once on this button to play a video

Beware

Video can take up a lot of storage space on your iPad. For instance, a one minute video takes up approximately 80 MB of storage.

Viewing Videos

As the name suggests, the Videos app can be used to download and view video content. This is from the iTunes Store, rather than viewing your own videos. To do this:

1 Tap once on this icon

2 The Videos app is initially empty of content. Tap once here to access video content in the iTunes Store, or tap once on the Store button

3 Tap once on the Films button or the TV Programmes button

4 Tap once on an item to review its content. Tap once here to download it. This is usually in the form of buying or renting a video

5 The downloaded video appears in the Videos app. Tap once on the cover to view its contents

6 Tap once here to play a video

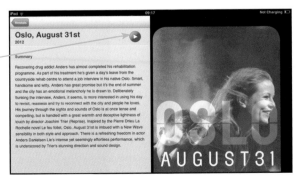

The buttons at the top of the Films window can be used to search for films by Featured, Top Chart or Genius, which offers suggestions based on what you have bought previously.

Don't forget

Don't forget

If you rent videos from the iTunes Store you have to watch them within 30 days. Once you have started watching the video you have to finish watching it within 48 hours. Once the rental period has expired, the video is deleted from your iPad.

Videos on YouTube

YouTube is a video sharing site that has become the starting point for most people when they want to find video content on the Web. It contains everything from music to instructional videos and it can be accessed on your iPad with the YouTube app:

1 Tap once on this icon

2 The latest video content is displayed with thumbnails

3 Use these buttons to navigate through the contents of the YouTube site

4 Use the Search box to find items with keywords

5 Tap once on a thumbnail to play the video. This plays at full screen size. Use these button to rewind, pause/ play or fast forward the video

Don't forget

To view a video within the YouTube interface i.e. not at full screen, tap once on this button on the playback toolbar. In this view there will be lists of other similar videos to the one that you are viewing.

Photo and Video Apps

Within the App Store there is a category for Photo & Video, offering a range of apps for capturing and editing photos and videos. Some to try are:

- iPhoto. This is the iPad version of the popular Apple photo editing and organizing app. It is part of the iLife suite of apps and can be used as a photo library and also for a range of editing techniques, creating slideshows and sharing your photos

- Adobe Photoshop Express. A mobile version of the bestselling Photoshop suite of video editing apps. Multi-Touch Gestures can be used to apply a range of editing techniques including artistic filters

- PowerCam HD. A camera app that can be used to capture both photos and videos. Different special effects can be applied when the photos or videos are captured

- 360 Panorama. This is an app that can be used to stitch your photos together to create a 360 degree view

- Photo Collage HD. An app for creating attractive collages with your photos. You can select and edit photos and add them to a collage with a range of backgrounds. It can then be shared via Facebook or Twitter

- iMovie. Another app from the Apple iLife suite. This is used to edit video that you have captured. It offers functions to trim video, add transitions, captions, music and voiceovers. Once the video has been edited it can then be shared via YouTube, Facebook or iTunes

- Video Editor for FREE. A video editing app that, as the name suggests, is free and a reasonable alternative to iMovie in terms of editing functionality

- Video Downloader. A useful app that can be used to play most video formats through a browser interface

- Playable. Another app for playing a wide range of video formats on your iPad

Hot tip

The third app in the iLife suite is GarageBand. This is an app for creating your own music. It has a range of digital instruments that can be used to record tracks and also pre-recorded loops that can be added.

149

Discovering Art

It is always a pleasure to view works of art in real life, but the next best alternative is to be able to look at them on the high-resolution Retina display on your iPad. As far as viewing art there are two options:

- Apps that contain general information about museums and art galleries

- Apps that display the works belonging to museums and art galleries

In general, type the name of a museum or art gallery into the App Store Search box to see if there is an applicable app. Some apps to look at are:

- Guggenheim. Information and examples from the iconic museum in Bilbao

- London Museum. A general guide for finding museums in London. With an Internet connection it can be used to phone museums for booking

- Metropolitan Museum of Art. A guide to the New York museum including a very useful floor guide

- Musée du Louvre HD. High-resolution images and descriptions of the world famous art of the Lourve

- Museum Finder. A general museum app for locating establishments around the world

- Prado Museum Audio Guide. A comprehensive audio guide to the Prado Museum in Madrid, including descriptions of 50 famous paintings

- Uffizi. Maps and descriptions of the world famous museum in Florence, including maps, examples and descriptions of the works of art

Creating Pictures

If you want to branch out from just looking at works of art, you can try creating some of your own too. There is a range of drawing and painting apps that can be used to let your creative side run riot. Most of these function in a similar fashion in terms of creating pictures:

1 Drawing tools appear at the bottom of the app

2 Swipe from left to right to access different tool options and selections

3 Tap and swipe on the screen to create a picture

Don't forget

Most drawing and painting apps have an Undo function and also an eraser that can be used to remove unwanted items.

151

Some apps to try are:

- Brushes. One of the most powerful painting apps with a wide range of tools and features, including up to six layers in each painting and five blend modes

- Drawing Pad. Similar to Brushes, but at not such a high level. More suitable as a first options for iPad painting

- Inspire Pro. A wide range of blending features makes this one of the best painting apps around

- Learn to Draw. A drawing app that has tutorials for learning how to draw and also examples that can be used as templates and copied over

- SketchBook Express. A sketching app at a similar level to Brushes for painting

Cooking With Your iPad

Your iPad may not be quite clever enough to cook dinner for you, but there are enough cookery apps to ensure that you will never go without a good meal with your iPad at your side. Some to look at are:

- 170,000+ Recipes. As the name suggests, thousands of recipes to keep you busy in the kitchen for as long as you want. You can also store your grocery lists here

- AllRecipes. Enter a type of food, or dish, into the search box and see a variety of related recipes

- Cake Recipes. To get your mouth watering, this app has hundreds of cake ideas, from the simple to the exotic

- Green Kitchen. A must for vegetarians, with stylish and creative recipes for organic and vegetarian food

- iCake Italian. If you cannot make it to Italy, bring a bit of Italy to your home with these recipes for cakes, pastries and tiramisu

- Jamie's Recipes. An app featuring the recipes of the well-known chef Jamie Oliver

- Recipes Starter Kit. For the less experienced chefs, this is a good way to gain confidence in the kitchen

- Slow Cooker Recipes. Put your dish together with this app, leave it in the slow cooker and then enjoy it several hours later when ready

- Sweet Baking. As well as covering cakes and cookies this app also has recipes for a variety of breads

Staying Healthy

Most people are health conscious these days and the App Store has a category covering Health & Fitness. This includes apps about general fitness, healthy eating, relaxation and yoga. Some to try are:

- Calorie Counter and Diet Tracker. If you want to stick to a diet this app can help you along the way. You need to register, which is free, and then you can set your own diet plan and fitness profile

- Daily Workouts. Some of the exercise apps are for dedicated gym-goers. If you are looking for something a bit less extreme this app could fit the bill. A range of exercises that will keep you fit without the need to be a body builder

- Daily Yoga. Audio and video instructions for timed sessions and over 30 yoga poses

- Menu Planner. A dieting aid that enables you to create your own menu plans

- MyPilatesGuru. Use this app to work through over 80 pilates exercise sessions. You can also create your own sessions and save them to repeat

- Serenity. Over 30 videos and sound files to help you relax or fall asleep

- Sleep Pillow Ambiance. Everyone enjoys a good night's sleep and this app can help you achieve it. A collection of ambient sounds are played to help you relax and sleep

- Universal Breathing. Designed to promote slow breathing, to help with a range of health conditions including high blood pressure, migraines and asthma

Don't forget

There is also a Medical category in the App Store that contains a range of apps covering medical topics.

153

Beware

If you have a genuine medical complaint, get it checked out by your doctor, rather than trying to find a solution through an app or on the Web.

Playing Games

Although computer games may seem like the preserve of the younger generation this is definitely not the case. Not all computer games are of the shoot-em-up or racing variety and the App Store also contains puzzles and versions of popular board games. There are two ways to access games:

- Via the App Store under the Games category

- Via the Games Center built-in iPad app. This is usually used if you want to compare scores with other users or if you want to play games simultaneously with other online people in a multi-player game

Some games to try are:

- Chess. Pit your wits against this chess app. Various settings can be applied for each game such as the level of difficulty

- Checkers. Similar to the Chess app, but for Checkers (Draughts). Hints are also available to help develop your skills and knowledge

- Mahjong. A version of the popular Chinese game, but this is a matching game for single players, rather than playing with other people

- Scrabble. An iPad version of the best-selling word game that can be played with up to four people

- Solitaire. An old favorite, the card game where you have to build sequences and remove all of the cards

- Sudoku. The numbers game where you have to fill different grids with numbers 1-9, without having any of the same in a row or column

- Tetris. One of the original computer games, where you have to piece together falling shapes to make lines

- Words With Friends. Similar to Scrabble, an online word game, played with other users

Don't forget

As well as the games here, there is also a full range of other types of games in the App Store.

154

10 Getting on the Map

With an iPad, the Maps app and a Wi-Fi connection, the world is your oyster. This chapter shows how to find locations and directions.

Looking Around Maps

With the Maps app you need never again wonder about where a location is, or worry about getting directions to somewhere. As long as you are connected to Wi-Fi you will be able to do the following:

- Search maps around the world

- Find addresses

- Find famous buildings or landmarks

- Find the locations of the people in your Contacts app

- Get directions between different locations

- View traffic conditions

To ensure that the Maps app works most effectively, it has to be enabled for Location Services. To do this:

1 Tap once on the Settings app

2 Tap once on this link

3 Drag the Location Service button to On

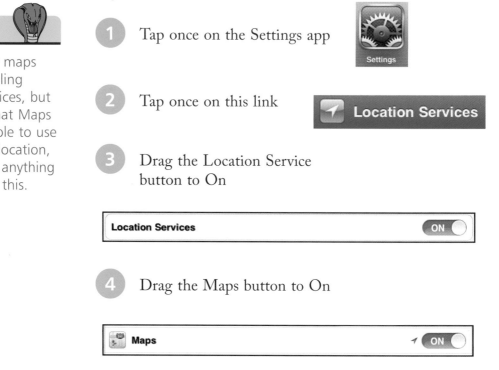

4 Drag the Maps button to On

Viewing maps

Once you have enabled Location Services you can start looking around maps:

 Tap once on this icon

 Tap once on this button to view your current location

Don't forget

You can also zoom in and out on maps by swiping outwards with thumb and forefinger, or pinching inwards, respectively.

Double-tap with one finger on a map to zoom in

Tap once with two fingers on a map to zoom out

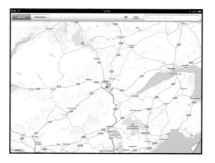

Finding Locations

Within Maps you can search for addresses, locations, landmarks, intersections or businesses. To do this:

1 Tap once on the Search button

 Search

2 Enter an item into the Search box

Q Sydney Harbour Bridge ☰

3 Tap once on the Search button on the keyboard

Search

Hot tip

You can also search for locations by post codes or zip codes.

4 The required item is identified and shown on a map. Pins are also dropped at this point

5 Locations can be viewed from a local, national or international level

Using Pins

Pins are used to identify locations and also display additional information about locations or addresses. They can also be used to access photos for a location.

In addition to pins that are dropped when you find a location you can also drop your own pins at any point. To use pins:

① Tap once on a pin to view its options

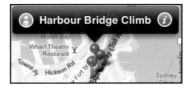

② Tap once on this button to view photos of the selected location

③ Tap once here to return to map view

④ Tap once on this button to access additional information about the selected item

⑤ Tap once on the phone number to make a FaceTime call or visit a website, if there is one. Tap once on these buttons to add an item to your Contacts, share it via email, iMessage or a tweet or add to your Safari bookmarks

Hot tip

To drop your own pin, tap and hold on a location. This drops a purple pin as opposed to the red ones. Tap and hold on a pin and drag it around to change its position.

Don't forget

Tap on the Directions buttons next to the thumbnail image to find directions to the selected location.

159

Getting Directions

Finding your way around is an important element of using maps and this can be done with the Directions function:

1 Tap once on the Directions button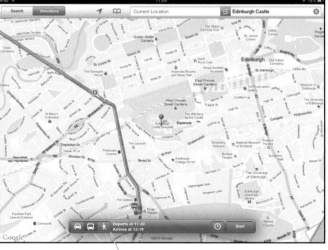

2 By default, your current direction is used for the From field. If you want to change this, tap once and enter a new location or address

3 Enter a destination location or address

4 Tap once on this button to swap the locations

5 Tap once on the Search button on the keyboard

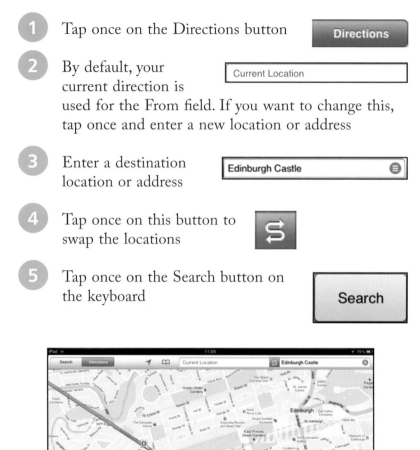

6 The destination location is shown on the map. Use this toolbar to view direction details

...cont'd

7   Tap once on the Start button to get directions

8   The route is shown on the map

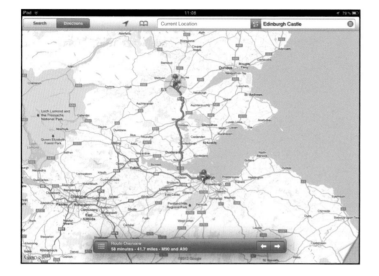

9   Tap once on this button to view details of the route for the selected mode of transport. The default option is by car

Don't forget

To get back to the Start view, tap once on the destination Search box and tap once on the Search button on the keyboard.

161

...cont'd

10 Tap once on this button to return to the map view

11 Tap once on these buttons to view directions step by step. On each tap, the directions advance one step

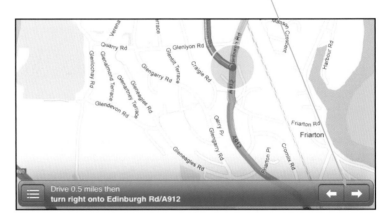

12 Tap once on this button to view the directions by Public transport

13 Tap once on this button to set times for your journey by public transport

14 Enter a departure time and tap once on the available options to view details

15 Tap once on this button to view the directions by foot

Finding Contacts

As well as looking for locations and landmarks, it is also possible to find locations and directions for people in your address book (Contacts app). To do this:

1 Tap once on this button

2 Tap once on a contact in your address book

3 If there is no address entered for the contact this will be displayed in the Info window

4 If there is an address associated with the contact, this will be displayed on a map and a pin will be dropped

Don't forget

Tap once on the image button on the pin toolbar, to see a photo of the contact's home or location.

163

Types of Maps

The standard view that is used in Maps can be changed so that you can view maps according to satellite, hybrid and terrain views. To do this:

 Swipe inwards here to access the map options

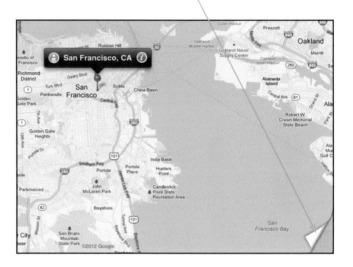

The Terms of Use can also be viewed in this area, by clicking on the link underneath the Overlays section.

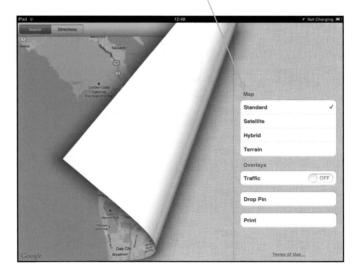 Select the map options here or swipe into the corner to return to map view

...cont'd

3 Tap once on the Satellite link to view a satellite image of the location

4 Tap once on the Hybrid link to view a combination of the standard view and the satellite view

Don't forget

Satellite, Hybrid and Terrain maps can be zoomed in and out on, in the same way as for the standard map view.

165

5 Tap once on the Terrain link to view a relief image of the location

Checking Traffic

Maps can also be used to display traffic information for locations. To do this:

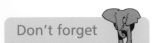

Don't forget

In the Overlays section there are also options for dropping a pin and printing the map.

Don't forget

To show traffic information you need to have an Internet connection.

 Access the Overlays section in the same way as for accessing the different map options on the previous two pages. Drag the Traffic button to On

Overlays	
Traffic	ON
Drop Pin	
Print	

The map is displayed with appropriate traffic details

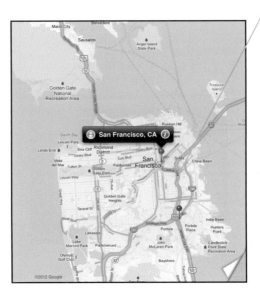

The following system is used for displaying traffic information:

- Green. Traffic moving according to appropriate speed limits

- Yellow. Traffic moving slower than appropriate speed limits

- Red. Issues leading to stop and go traffic

- Gray. No data available

11 Traveling Companion

This chapter shows why you should never be without your iPad when you are traveling or on vacation.

Traveling With Your iPad

When you go traveling, there are a few essentials that you have to consider: passport, money and insurance to name three. To this you can add your iPad: it is a perfect traveling companion that can help you plan your trip and keep you informed and entertained when you are away from home.

Uses for traveling

There are a lot of App Store apps that can be used for different aspects of traveling. However, the built-in apps can also be put to good use before and during your travels:

- Maps. Use this app for accessing maps of your destinations, finding directions and viewing images of areas to which you are traveling

- Notes. Create items such as lists of items to pack or landmarks that you want to visit

- Contacts. Keep your Contacts app up-to-date so that you can use it to send postcards to friends and family. You can also use it to access phone numbers if you want to phone home

- Reminders. Set reminders for important tasks, such as changing foreign currency, buying tickets and details of flights

- Music. Use this app to play your favorite music while you are traveling, or relaxing at your destination

- Photos. Store photos of your trip with this app and play them back as a slideshow when you get back home

- FaceTime. If you have a Wi-Fi connection at your destination you will be able to keep in touch with video calls (as long as the recipient has FaceTime too)

- iBooks. Instead of dragging lots of heavy books around, use this app for your holiday library

Beware

You can also use the Videos app to download movies and TV shows from the iTunes Store. However, these will take up a significant amount of space on your iPad in terms of storage.

Planning Your Trip

A lot of the fun of going on vacation and traveling is in the planning. The anticipation of researching new places to visit and explore can whet the appetite for what is ahead. The good news is that you can plan your whole itinerary while sitting in an armchair with your iPad by your side. In the App Store there are apps for organizing your itinerary and others for exploring the possibilities of where you can go:

Tripit

This is an app for keeping all of your travel details in one place. You have to register, which is free, and you can then enter your own itinerary details. Whenever you receive an email confirmation for a flight, hotel or car hire that you have booked, you can email this to your Tripit account (plans@tripit.com) and this will be added to your itinerary.

GetPacked

A great way to get peace of mind before you leave. This app generates a packing list and to-do lists to check before you leave, based on questions that you answer about your

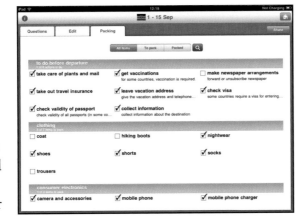

vacation and travel arrangements. You can then select items to include on your packing list, from clothes to documents and medical items.

Don't forget

Although there is a small fee for the GetPacked app, it is well worth it as it covers everything you will need to consider before you leave.

...cont'd

Cool Escapes

Guaranteed to give you itchy feet, this app matches quality hotels with some amazing locations around the world. You can explore by map, country, area, hotel type and price, to find the perfect combination.

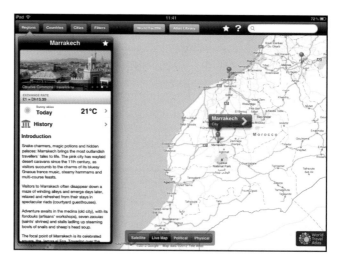

World Travel Atlas

A comprehensive travel companion that offers a world atlas that contains information about countries, cities, landmarks, airports and events. Navigate around the atlas with the same swiping and tapping gestures as with the Maps app. Tap once on an item to access a wealth of information about it.

Beware

Some maps apps are free to initially download but there is then a fee to buy the associated maps.

Viewing Flights

Flying is a common part of modern life and although you do not have to book separate flights for a vacation (if it is part of a package) there are a number of apps for booking flights and also following the progress of those in the air:

Skyscanner

This app can be used to find flights at airports around the world. Enter your details such as leaving airport, destination and dates of travel. The results show a range of available options, covering different price ranges.

FlightRadar24

If you like viewing the path of flights that are in the air, or need to check to see if flights are going to be delayed, this app provides this inflight information. Flights are shown according to flight number and airline.

AirportZoom

As well as showing real-time flight details, this app also has airline departure and arrival information and maps of airport terminals and flight gates.

FlightAware

Another app for tracking flights, showing arrivals and departures and also information about delays.

Finding Hotels

The Internet is a perfect vehicle for finding good value hotel rooms around the world. When hotels have spare capacity, this can quickly be relayed to associated websites, where users can usually benefit from cheap prices and special offers. There are plenty of apps that have details of thousands of hotels around the world, such as:

TripAdvisor
One of the top travel apps, this not only has hotel information but also restaurant, activities and flights. Enter a destination in the search box and then navigate through the available options.

Hotels.com
A stylish app that enables you to enter search keywords or tap once on a hotel on the homescreen to view options for this location.

172

Hot tip

Most hotel apps have reviews of all of the listed establishments. It is always worth reading these as it gives you a view from the people who have actually been there.

Booking.com
Another good, fully featured hotel app that provides a comprehensive service and excellent prices.

iRooms@LateRooms.com
An app that specializes in getting the best prices by dealing with rooms that are available at short notice. Some genuine bargains can be found here, for hotels of all categories.

Converting Currency

Money is always important in life and never more so than when you are on vacation and possibly following a budget. It is therefore imperative to know the exchange rate of currencies in different countries compared to your own. Two apps that provide this service are:

XE Currency

This app delivers information about exchange rates for all major world currencies and also a wealth of background information such as high and low rates and historical charts.

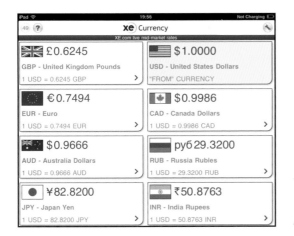

When changing currency, either at home or abroad, always shop around to get the best rate. Using credit cards abroad usually attracts a supplementary charge too.

Currency

This app provides up-to-date exchange rates for over 150 currencies and 100 countries.

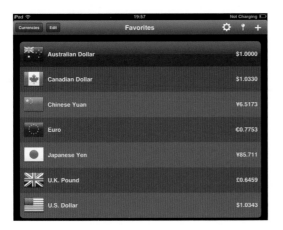

Travel Apps

Everyone has different priorities and preferences when they are on vacation. The following are some apps from the App Store that cover a range of activities and services:

- 1000 Places To See Before You Die. A collection of stunning and unforgettable destinations and locations around the world. Impressive photography makes it all the more appealing and you can also browse maps

- Disneyland Paris. If you are entertaining your grandchildren at Disneyland Paris, this app will help you survive the experience. Maps, show times, descriptions of features help you organize all aspects of your visit

- Fotopedia Heritage. A selection of stunning photography of World Heritage sites. Guaranteed to make you want to head for the airport

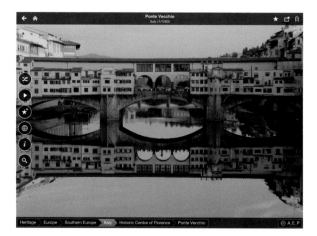

- Florida Theme Parks. Another one for the family and grandchildren. Everything you need to know about these popular tourist attractions

- Google Earth. Not just a travel aid, this app enables you to search around the globe and look at photos and 3D maps of your favorite places

- Hailo. For anyone visiting London, this app allows you to hail a cab, just at the tap of a button

- Kayak. A useful all-round app that compares hundreds of travel websites to get the best prices for flights, hotels and car rental. You can also create your own itineraries

- Language apps. If you want to learn a new language for your travels, there is a wide range of apps for this. These are located in either the Travel or Education categories in the App Store

- myLanguage Free Translator. If you do not have the time, or inclination, to learn a new language, try this app to translate 59 different languages

- New York Subway Map. Use this app to help get around the Big Apple via the Subway. Plan your journeys and view live updates about stations and routes

Don't forget

There are apps for displaying train times and details, but these are usually specific to your geographical location rather than covering a range of different countries.

- Open Table. Eating out is an important part of being on vacation and this app helps simplify the process by detailing over 20,000 restaurants in the USA, Canada and the UK, where you can review the menus and make table reservations for free

- Over 40 Magnifier and Flashlight. Not just for traveling, this fantastic app acts as a torch and a magnifying glass all in one

- P&O Cruises. Find some of your favorite cruises with this app that displays the full brochure of P&O Cruises

...cont'd

Beware

The Phrasebook app comes with one free language. After that you have to pay a small fee for each language that you want to use.

- Paris Transport Map. One free map for travel options around one of the great cities in the world

- Photo Translator. Ever wondered what signs in a foreign language mean? This app can translate them for you: take a photo with your iPad and the app gives you a translation of the sign, or phrase

- Phrasebook. Keep up with what the locals are saying in different countries with this app that has useful phrases in 25 languages

- Sixt Rent a Car. Use this app for car rental in 90 countries around the world

- London Tube Map. Find your way around London with this digital version of the icon Tube Map. It includes live departure boards and station information

- Urbanspoon. Another app for finding restaurants on your vacation. Enter your location, shake your iPad and the app uses a slot machine interface to come up with suggestions. Covers USA, Canada, UK and Australia

- Wi-Fi Finder. It is always useful to be able to access Wi-Fi when you are on vacation, and sometimes essential. This app locates Wi-Fi hotspots in 650,000 locations in 144 countries worldwide

- Word Lens. Similar to Photo Translator, this is another app for translating foreign signs, phrases or menus. The app is free to download but the language packs have to then be bought separately

- World Clock. View the time in six cities around the world, including an icon of a landmark in that city. For a small fee there is a paid-for version that includes a wider range of world cities

- Yelp. Covering a range of services, this app locates restaurants, shops, services and places of interest in cities around the world

12 Practical Matters

This chapter looks at security issues on the iPad and also shows how to use it for financial issues and buying property.

Setting Restrictions

Within the iPad Settings app there are options for restricting types of content that can be viewed and also actions that can be performed. These include:

- Turning off certain apps so that they cannot be used

- Enabling changes to certain functions

- Restricting content that is viewed using specific apps

When setting restrictions, they can be locked so that no-one else can change them. To set and lock restrictions:

① Tap once on the Settings app

② Tap once on the General tab

③ Tap once on the Restrictions link

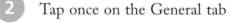

| Restrictions | Off › |

④ The restrictions are greyed-out, i.e. they have not been enabled for use yet

Allow:	
Safari	ON
YouTube	ON
Camera	ON
FaceTime	ON

⑤ Tap once on the Enable Restrictions link

Enable Restrictions

Hot tip

It is a good idea to set up some restrictions on your iPad if grandchildren are going to have access to it.

6 Type on the keypad to set a passcode for enabling and disabling restrictions

7 Re-enter the passcode

8 All of the Restrictions options become available. Drag these buttons On or Off to disable certain apps. If this is done they will no longer be visible on the Home screen. Tap once on the links under Allowed Content to specify restrictions for certain types of content, such as music, movies and apps

Finding Your iPad

No-one likes to think the worst, but if your iPad is lost or stolen, help is at hand. The Find My iPad function (operated through the iCloud service) allows you to send a message and an alert to a lost iPad and also remotely lock it or even wipe its contents. This gives added peace of mind, knowing that even if your iPad is lost or stolen its contents will not necessarily be compromised. To set up Find My iPad:

 Tap once on the Settings app

 Tap once on the iCloud link

Drag this button to On to be able to find your iPad on a map and send messages to it remotely

Tap once on the Allow button to enable the Find My iPad functionality

Finding a lost iPad

Once you have set up Find My iPad you can search for it through the iCloud service. To do this:

Login to your iCloud account at www.icloud.com

 Tap once on the Find My iPhone button (this also works for the iPad)

3 Your iPad is identified and its current location is shown on a map

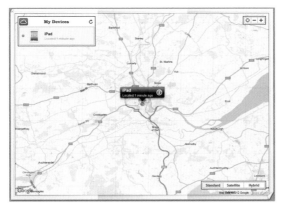

4 Tap once on the blue i symbol to access the Find My iPad functionality

5 Tap once here to send a sound alert and a message to your iPad

Don't forget

Tap once on the Remote Lock button to lock the iPad and tap once on the Remote Wipe button to delete the iPad's contents.

6 Type a message and drag this button to the On position to play an alert sound on your iPad too. Tap once on the Send button to send the message and sound

Don't forget

When you send a message to your iPad you also receive an email to your iCloud email account to confirm that it is you who has sent the message and alert.

7 The message appears on the locked screen of the iPad

Important Message
Hi I've misplaced my iPad somewhere. If you are reading this could you phone on 07865123456

Locking Your iPad

As shown in Chapter Two, the screen can be auto-locked, but this does not have a security control. If you want to make sure that no-one else can access your iPad's content a passcode can be set for unlocking the screen. To do this:

1 Tap once on the Settings app

2 Tap once on the General link

3 Tap once on the Passcode Lock button

> Passcode Lock   Off >

4 Tap once on the Turn Passcode On link

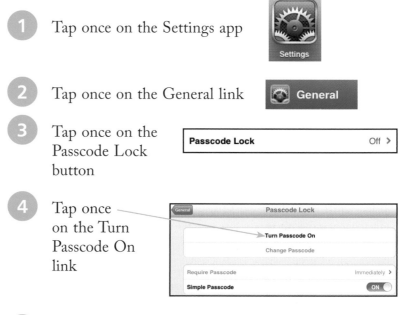

Don't forget

Once the passcode has been set, tap once on the Require Passcode button to specify when the passcode is activated. This can be immediately, or over a period of time.

5 Enter the passcode and re-enter it to confirm it

6 The passcode has to be entered to access the iPad for use every time it has been locked

Avoiding Viruses

As far as security from viruses on the iPad is concerned there is good news and bad news:

- The good news is that, due to its architecture, most apps on the iPad do not communicate with each other so, even if there was a virus, it is unlikely that it would infect the whole iPad. Also, there are relatively few viruses being aimed at the iPad, particularly compared to those for Windows PCs

- The bad news is that no computer system is immune from viruses and malware and complacency is one of the biggest enemies of computer security. Also, as iPads become more popular they will become a more attractive target for hackers and virus writers

iPad security

Apple takes security on the iPad very seriously and one way that this manifests itself is in the fact it is designed so that different apps do not talk to each other. This means that if there was a virus in an app then it would be hard for it to transfer to others and therefore spread across the iPad. Apple's own apps are the exception to this, but as they are developed and checked by Apple there is very little chance of them being infected by viruses.

Antivirus options

There are a few apps in the App Store that deal with antivirus issues, although not actually removing viruses, due to the lack of iPad viruses in circulation. Some options to look at:

- VirusBarrier. This checks files that are copied onto your iPad, via email or online services, to ensure that they are virus-free

- McAfee Global Threat Intelligence Mobile. This is not technically an antivirus app, but it does provide a daily update about new viruses that are in circulation

- Anti-Virus Detective. This is an app that has a step-by-step process for identifying suspected viruses or malware

Don't forget

Malware is short for malicious software, designed to harm your computer or access and distribute information from it.

Don't forget

Apple also check apps that are provided through the App Store and this process is very robust. This does not mean that it is impossible for a virus to infect the iPad (but there have not been any so far) so keep an eye on the Apple website to see if there are any details about iPad viruses.

Dealing With Money

We all like to keep track of our money and, although it may not be as much fun as reading books or looking at photos, it is a necessary task, that can be undertaken on the iPad.

Some general financial apps are looked at on page 186, but one of the most common uses for financial matters is online banking. This is where you can use banking apps to access you bank accounts.

Banking apps are specific to your geographical location i.e. the banks that operate in your country. Most banking apps operate in a similar way:

Beware

If you are logging into your online banking service, make sure any Remember Me login details functions are checked off, particularly if other people have access to your iPad.

Don't forget

Online banking sites can also be accessed through the Web using Safari.

1 You have to first register for the online service. Once you have done this tap on the Log On button to access your account details

2 General information is also available through the app such as branch locations and contact details

Looking at Property

If you are looking to move home, or buy property as an investment, your iPad is a great starting point. There are a lot of real estate apps that provide high quality color photos of all parts of properties for sale.

As with banking apps, real estate apps are specific to your geographical location and they all have a search facility for looking for properties in different areas. The search results can usually be filtered by criteria such as price, number of bedrooms and property type. To use a real estate app:

 Browse properties according to area

Don't forget

Some property apps also allow you to book appointments to view properties in person.

Tap once on a property to view more details. This usually includes photos of all of the rooms and a full description of the property

Financial Apps

Within the Finance category of the App Store there are apps for managing your personal finances, viewing share prices and organizing your bank accounts and bills. Some to look at are:

- Account Tracker. A useful app for keeping track of your expenditure. It can be used to monitor multiple bank accounts and also set alerts and reminders for pay bills

- Calculator. For working out your own finances, this calculator provides a large, attractive interface with plenty of functionality

- Bloomberg. This is an app for following stocks and shares. You can add any shares that you own and view live prices while markets are open (with a 15 minute delay). There is also a news service with related financial details

- HomeBudget. An app for managing your household incomes and expenses. It also supports charts and graphs so you can compare expenditure over periods of time

- Meter Readings. Useful for keeping an eye on your fuel consumption, this app helps you to save money by monitoring your utility readings. Enter the readings and your usage and costs are displayed in user-friendly graphs to show where savings can be made

- Mint.com. Another general finance app for managing your money and monitoring budgets

- Money for iPad Free. As well as being used to manage bills and view all of your accounts, this app also provides useful planning features and reminders

- Pocket Expense. Another in the range of apps with which you can monitor bank accounts, track bills, view transactions and see where you can save money

- SharePrice. Another app for seeing how your share portfolio is doing. Real-time share information, market news and profit/loss details are provided

Hot tip

With your iPad and an Internet connection, you should always be able to keep an eye on your shares portfolio as well as buying and selling shares, wherever you are.

Index

189

190

191